" The Object Lessons series achieves something very close to magic: the books take ordinary—even banal—objects and animate them with a rich history of invention, political struggle, science, and popular mythology. Filled with fascinating details and conveyed in sharp, accessible prose, the books make the everyday world come to life. Be warned: once you've read a few of these, you'll start walking around your house, picking up random objects, and musing aloud: 'I wonder what the story is behind this thing?'"

Steven Johnson, author of *Where Good Ideas Come From* and *How We Got to Now*

" Object Lessons describes themselves as 'short, beautiful books,' and to that, I'll say, amen. . . . If you read enough Object Lessons books, you'll fill your head with plenty of trivia to amaze and annoy your friends and loved ones—caution recommended on pontificating on the objects surrounding you. More importantly, though . . . they inspire us to take a second look at parts of the everyday that we've taken for granted. These are not so much lessons about the objects themselves, but opportunities for self-reflection and storytelling. They remind us that we are surrounded by a wondrous world, as long as we care to look."

John Warner, *The Chicago Tribune*

T0315417

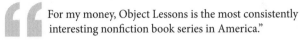

For my money, Object Lessons is the most consistently interesting nonfiction book series in America."

Megan Volpert, *PopMatters*

Besides being beautiful little hand-sized objects themselves, showcasing exceptional writing, the wonder of these books is that they exist at all . . . Uniformly excellent, engaging, thought-provoking, and informative."

Jennifer Bort Yacovissi,
Washington Independent Review of Books

. . . edifying and entertaining . . . perfect for slipping in a pocket and pulling out when life is on hold."

Sarah Murdoch, *Toronto Star*

Though short, at roughly 25,000 words apiece, these books are anything but slight."

Marina Benjamin, *New Statesman*

[W]itty, thought-provoking, and poetic . . . These little books are a page-flipper's dream."

John Timpane, *The Philadelphia Inquirer*

"The joy of the series, of reading *Remote Control, Golf Ball, Driver's License, Drone, Silence, Glass, Refrigerator, Hotel,* and *Waste* . . . in quick succession, lies in encountering the various turns through which each of their authors has been put by his or her object. . . . The object predominates, sits squarely center stage, directs the action. The object decides the genre, the chronology, and the limits of the study. Accordingly, the author has to take her cue from the *thing* she chose or that chose her. The result is a wonderfully uneven series of books, each one a *thing* unto itself."

Julian Yates, *Los Angeles Review of Books*

"The Object Lessons series has a beautifully simple premise. Each book or essay centers on a specific object. This can be mundane or unexpected, humorous or politically timely. Whatever the subject, these descriptions reveal the rich worlds hidden under the surface of things."

Christine Ro, *Book Riot*

". . . a sensibility somewhere between Roland Barthes and Wes Anderson."

Simon Reynolds, author of *Retromania: Pop Culture's Addiction to Its Own Past*

OBJECT LESSONS

A book series about the hidden lives of ordinary things.

Series Editors:

Ian Bogost and Christopher Schaberg

Advisory Board:

Sara Ahmed, Jane Bennett, Jeffrey Jerome Cohen, Johanna Drucker, Raiford Guins, Graham Harman, renée hoogland, Pam Houston, Eileen Joy, Douglas Kahn, Daniel Miller, Esther Milne, Timothy Morton, Kathleen Stewart, Nigel Thrift, Rob Walker, Michele White

In association with

BOOKS IN THE SERIES

TV

SUSAN BORDO

BLOOMSBURY ACADEMIC
NEW YORK • LONDON • OXFORD • NEW DELHI • SYDNEY

BLOOMSBURY ACADEMIC
Bloomsbury Publishing Inc
1385 Broadway, New York, NY 10018, USA
50 Bedford Square, London, WC1B 3DP, UK
29 Earlsfort Terrace, Dublin 2, Ireland

BLOOMSBURY, BLOOMSBURY ACADEMIC and the Diana logo are trademarks of Bloomsbury
Publishing Plc

First published in the United States of America 2021

Library of Congress Cataloging-in-Publication Data

Names: Bordo, Susan, 1947, author.
Title: TV / Susan Bordo.
Other titles: Television
Description: New York : Bloomsbury Academic, 2021. | Series: Object lessons
| Includes bibliographical references. | Summary: "Personal memoir meets
television history in a look back at how TV has changed, and how it has
also changed us, over the past seven decades"– Provided by publisher.
Identifiers: LCCN 2020039635 | ISBN 9781501362521 (paperback) | ISBN
9781501362538 (epub) | ISBN 9781501362545 (pdf)
Subjects: LCSH: Television broadcasting–United States–History. |
Television broadcasting–Social aspects–United States. | Baby boom
generation. | Feminist theory.
Classification: LCC PN1992.3.U5 B67 2021 | DDC 791.450973–dc23
LC record available at https://lccn.loc.gov/2020039635

ISBN: PB: 978-1-5013-6252-1
ePDF: 978-1-5013-6254-5
eBook: 978-1-5013-6253-8

Series: Object Lessons

Typeset by Deanta Global Publishing Services, Chennai, India
Printed and bound in Great Britain

To find out more about our authors and books visit www.bloomsbury.com
and sign up for our newsletters.

For my family: Edward, Cassie, Mickey, Binnie, and Scott.

CONTENTS

PREFACE

The title of this series is "Object Lessons." It's been a long time, however, since the word "television" conjured an object in the material sense. In the 1940s, 10-inch screens could be encased in enormous mahogany cabinets that might include a record player and a radio—truly part of a "set"—and people considered the quality of the wood and design of the "box" as important as the reception, which was pretty poor no matter what brand you chose. In 2020, the word "box" has lingered, but only as slang, and the elaborate wooden "sets" don't exist except in antique stores or grandparents' attics. People ignore aesthetics in favor of the pragmatics of screen size and definition. At one end, they might hang a huge HD flat screen on top of a gorgeous fireplace that other generations would make the centerpiece of the room. On the other end, younger people enjoy movies and television series on their smartphones. In 2020, "television" is *what* we watch, not the material object we watch it on.

One of my favorite movies, Barry Levinson's *Avalon* (1990), uses changing relations to television as a material trope to chronicle changing social relations within an immigrant Jewish family in post–Second World War Baltimore. When it first arrives, the television is an exciting novelty, around which the entire Krichinsky clan gathers, spellbound by the technology itself, patiently waiting two-and-a-half hours for the Indian Head test pattern to give way to an actual show. Skip ahead in time, and television, like going out to the movies, becomes a scheduled entertainment for the family but not yet an intrusion into their cohesion, as they all stay together when dinner is over to share a favorite show. Eventually, however, the family is eating Swanson ready-made dinners, staring at the set without any conversation among them. A parallel narrative charts a move to "the suburbs" (deliberately generic, that exotic other land of space and green), the grandparents moving into their own place, and ultimately a fragmentation of the extended family's ritual meal at Thanksgiving.

Much of *Avalon* was familiar to me. When I was growing up, watching television was something that brought our (not very cohesive) family together. Whatever else we were doing, we'd hear the friendly men from Texaco announcing Uncle Miltie or Dina Shore singing "See the USA in Your Chevrolet" or the theme music from *I Love Lucy* and it would be a signal to stop whatever else we might be doing and gather. We were one of the first on the block to get a set, and it conferred great prestige on us. We were the kind of family that CBS set designer Willard Levitas has in mind as he recollects: "You would see the RCA truck parked on the street and everyone would say 'they've got a TV'. Then, when Berle came on, the street would literally be deserted . . . Every house with a TV, there would be a crowd. You didn't invite, but you couldn't say no."[1]

In contrast, my daughter doesn't even watch "the box," much less hang with us. While we are watching TV, she's in her room with her phone. She lives on YouTube videos of animal rescues, vehicular near-disasters, and make-up lessons from insanely beautiful young people of indeterminate gender. Like others who have totally cut the cord to cable, she does watch some Netflix—sometimes the same movies or show her father and I are viewing downstairs. But she'd never describe what she's doing as "watching television." I wonder how this alters the experience for her. For me, whether in a darkened theatre or lying on my couch binging on *Downton Abbey*, I am deliciously immersed, not so different from the way I became immersed in *Little Women* when I was a preteen. Surroundings disappear, a different reality takes over; how can that possibly happen through the miniature world of the iPhone?

I asked my daughter Cassie. "Gen Z is a really anxious and depressed generation," she replied, "and we like putting on our earphones, focusing on one small thing, and making everything else go away." In some ways, not so different after all from my experience growing up—and in other ways very different, particularly when it comes to the "everything else" she is trying to make go away.

This book will not be a survey of how television programming has changed over the years. That, particularly if it included a full range of genres, would be an encyclopedic project. My emphasis will be on my experience as a baby boomer born in 1947, just as television was becoming available to consumers. Television and I grew up together—and from the beginning, TV exerted a powerful influence on my life. It did, as well, on a man just a few months older than I, and managed to raise him to a prominence that has very nearly destroyed American Democracy—always flawed but never assaulted so brazenly and corruptly. TV as I knew it growing up and the rise (and perhaps, as you are reading this, fall) of what some have called a reality-show presidency are the beginning and end points of this book. In between are reflections on how the anxieties and excitements of my generation, the cultural and political movements that we experienced (as well as backlash against them) became increasingly instrumental in shaping what programmers were willing to take a chance on, what counter-programming sprung up, what caught on and what withered away. I hope that the interweaving of my own story and the televisual moments that stand out for me will illustrate what a constant companion and dominant force—for good and for bad—television has been in carrying us to the present moment. As such, it will also have a lot to say about what brought us to Donald Trump and the "everything else" my daughter tries to escape, as she focuses on that tiny screen in her darkened bedroom.

1 WAITING FOR JOSEPH WELCH

"We were used by [him], but that's the nature of reporting and television especially. It was a terrible dilemma. I'm sure every responsible news office in the country was worrying, 'How the hell do you handle this kind of stuff when you know the son of a bitch is lying?'

You have to say what the guy is saying, but we couldn't catch up with his lies fast enough before another one came out, so we were giving him this buildup. The more you wrote about him, even attacked him, the more powerful he became. This is what demagoguery is all about. The hope is eventually you catch up with the truth, but meanwhile the devastation that takes place lasts a long time."

Joseph Wershba, *See It Now* reporter, on Joseph McCarthy

FIGURE 1 Watching the Army–McCarthy Hearings in April 1954 while doing women's work. Everett Collection Historical/Alamy.

As I revisit my experience of television, I'm struck by the fact that my earliest memories and what is playing on my living room TV at this very moment are cultural bookends, beginning with the moment when TV helped bring down an authoritarian bully and ending with an authoritarian bully created and elevated *by* TV.

When you grow up with television, however, memory can be tricky. Did you see Oswald shot by Jack Ruby as it happened, live on TV? Or has your own experience become enmeshed with the mythologizing of that moment? I know I saw Oswald shot because my father and I were watching television together at the time. "Daughter"—he called me that when he was about to say something of great moment—"you just watched history made before your eyes." Over the next few days, we saw that history made over and over, which was a novelty in itself. Replays—groaningly frequent—are now standard stuff in a 24-hour news cycle. How could they fill up the time without them? The anchors have difficulty managing the few minutes of banter they are required to perform with each other now; in the fifties, however, the evening news was only on once a day, and it took a truly extraordinary event to interrupt regular programming with replays.

So I know I saw Oswald being shot. But I'm not so sure about the McCarthy hearings. I would have been six-and-a-half years old, so I undoubtedly didn't understand any of it; I would have been engrossed in something else—coloring, maybe, trying hard to stay inside the lines and create the masterpiece that I always expected of myself, searching for the burnt sienna crayon. Still, in some dim way I must have heard the famous words:

> *Until this moment, Senator, I think I never really gauged your cruelty or your recklessness . . . Senator, may we not drop this? We know he belonged to the Lawyer's Guild . . . Let us not assassinate this lad further, Senator; you've done enough. Have you no sense of decency, sir, at long last? Have you left no sense of decency?*[1]

When I scrutinize this memory, though, I find lots of reasons why it was implausible that I heard it as it happened. It was a

Wednesday—June 9, 1954 to be exact—so my father would have been at "the place" (factory) in Brooklyn or downtown Newark, or more likely on the road, meeting with brokers in upstate New York. He loved politics, but my mother would have been watching *Search for Tomorrow* or *The Guiding Light*. And that day—the day that Joseph Welch socked it to McCarthy and turned the tide of the hearings—was June 9; wouldn't I have been at school? After decades of watching political documentaries and teaching iconic televisual moments to my students, I can't really be sure if I heard Joseph Welch demolish McCarthy as it happened. What I am sure of is that that moment is a standout in any narrative I would construct of my life as a television viewer.

Today, I long for another moment like that, which with one blow would send the edifice of authoritarianism crashing down—or expose a President's corruption, as we had witnessed during the televised final six days of the House Judiciary Committee's deliberations over Nixon's impeachment. When the Committee brought three articles of impeachment against Nixon and the House voted to have the entire impeachment trial televised, Nixon resigned in a prime-time television address. He saw the cards for indictment were on the table. But also, after his fatal, sweaty showing during the Kennedy debates, he had learned to respect the power of television and the damage a televised trial could do to any standing he might retain in the history books.

At one point, we thought Robert Mueller might provide our Joseph Welch moment: The Report that would expose

Trump once and for all. We waited and waited, and one of the digital savvy among us put together a startlingly realistic video spin on "The Untouchables," in which Mueller, like some modern-day Elliot Ness, collared all the crooks from Flynn to Trump. Our pulses quickened and our hearts gladdened when we heard The Report was about to be released. But Mueller, bless him, thought history was still written with a quill pen. He actually expected Americans to read 400 pages of dense prose and do the right thing by it. He didn't "get" television at all. But disastrously, Donald Trump and his Attorney General Bill Barr, following the Roger Ailes playbook, did. Trump and Barr understood that the phrase "No collusion," said often enough before a viewing audience, could easily defeat evidence and argument.[2]

Watching Bill Barr replace Mueller's painstakingly prepared, factually impeccable report with televised lies was especially deflating for those of us left-wing boomers whose politics had been grounded in the written word: Marx, The Port Huron Manifesto, Herbert Marcuse. Yet we are also children of television, so we harbored the fantasy of a politically explosive report delivered by a hero who, in a devastating moment of televised honesty and courage, would save us from our increasingly surreal "normalcy." TV, as we were growing up, was full of transforming moments like that, both fictional and real. We weren't ready for the possibility that the same televisual world that helped end a war via images of burning monks and fallen student protesters would also give us . . . Donald Trump.

2 WE HAVE SIX TELEVISIONS

Are you surprised? Do you imagine that because I am a critic of popular culture I wouldn't be caught dead watching *Dance Moms*? If so, you've been reading too many academics who came to popular culture only after it became Europeanized and hot. When I was in graduate school, the voracious maw of theory had only begun to invade and chew up the objects of everyday life into unrecognizable form. There were as yet no popular culture departments, the closest you could get was film studies—within which you could study *Nosferatu* but not *Jaws*.

I was in philosophy because I loved history, was fascinated by the play of ideas in historical time, and enjoyed taking texts apart, foraging for their meanings. I was good with words, and I was a good arguer. It seemed a better place for me than any of the other disciplines. But my heart was elsewhere—it just hadn't yet found a home in academia—and because I hadn't the financial resources to strike out as a writer and these were the days when becoming a college teacher was still a fairly reliable path to earning a steady income, that's what I did.

I also loved teaching. But I was frustrated by the bridge that I had to cross to make community with my students. Then one day I hit on the idea of asking them to write about how they experienced the duality of mind and body in their own lives—and discovered that Descartes was living right there, in their hatred of jiggling flesh and exaltation of their own will power to say "I can defeat you" to the cravings of their bodies.

Before long they were bringing in Nike "Just Do It" ads, talking about how Jennifer Aniston had been chubby as a child, and the bridge between the seventeenth century and the twentieth was crossed. And so, too, had the bridge between the future of my scholarship and my own experience: those things that I felt I truly knew about, having lived every day of my life with them—movies! television! magazines! commercials! The way they reflect and transform cultural change, and the way humans see themselves.

In short: I was not an academic who started out in the archives and gravitated toward popular culture when it became an accepted field of study. I was a popular culture fiend who went into academia because there was nowhere else for me to go—and discovered that the time was right for a marriage between my deepest interests and the latest thing in scholarship.

So, I don't have six televisions because they are required for my work (although that's what the IRS thinks). I have six televisions because I love television. I also hate television. But I've never found those two to be incompatible.

Here's where my televisions live:

One is in the porch turned family room, where my treadmill lives. The treadmill was moved from the basement when my husband had cancer; a runner and bicyclist, he wanted to keep exercising while he recovered, but the mildewy basement wasn't the place for a compromised immune system. So our lovely enclosed sunroom, surrounded by beautiful bushes and full of light, became a television room, where I now accumulate my daily steps quota with Netflix, Hulu or Amazon Prime.

We have a TV in the guest bedroom. And there's one in my office, which is on just about all the time. Yes, I write with the television on. I learned how to do this growing up. Born in 1947, I can't remember a time when television wasn't a constant part of my life. Always eager to assimilate his immigrant roots to American life, my father was the first in our neighborhood to buy a TV, and it was always on.

There's a huge television in the basement, a holdover from the days when my daughter played video games. No one has watched it since the room became trashed by Cassie and her live-in friend with half-drunk Ale-8s and old Reese's wrappers.

The smallest television is in the bedroom my husband and I share. It's the smallest because we only share the room marginally, given our vastly different sleeping and waking habits (I'm usually awake at 5:30, and am nodding off while he stealthily switches the channel to a sports event). Beyond sports, my husband rarely cares about what's on the screen. He was born before the war, to a family of lawyers and founders of Cornell University. He grew up without television. Thus, it's only a peripheral habit for him; he "watches" with headphones on, reading French newspapers on his laptop, learning new phrases, or practicing piano on his silent keyboard. When I ask him what he wants to watch as I scan the Netflix offerings, he rarely has preferences. "A British crime drama" is the most specific he gets—or one of the Jason Bourne movies. He'd be happy to watch one of those every day.

The most important television in our home is in the living room. That's where my husband and I sit in the evening, watching MSNBC, shouting obscenities at pundits and politicians. It's also where I often drift to sleep under a huge quilt, my three dogs nestled against (read: shoving) various parts of my body, unable to move myself to go to bed despite the fact that I've been relegated by Piper, Dakota, and Sean to about one quarter of the available space of the couch. It's shaped my body into a permanent pretzel, and I've tried to wean myself of this habit, but like Toni Morrison's Beloved, I can't be evicted from that magnetic spot, not even by myself. My husband turns down the volume as he goes upstairs but I often wake in the middle of the night to the second round of Rachel Maddow in the background. The strangest thing: I sometimes wake at exactly the place where I nodded off during the nine o'clock show. It's as though my television is keeping track of me.

Why can't I move from the couch to the bedroom? Partly it's the quilt—put me under a cozy enough one and I'm two years old again. Partly it's the doggies, whose warm breath reassures me that sweetness and innocent, creaturely love still survives. But also—I simply can't drag myself away from the television. To do so is to create a vacuum of dread for me. I've skewered broadcast news more ruthlessly than any other critic; yet at 10 p.m. the anchors become familiar, intimate friends whom I can't bear to abandon. Or perhaps more precisely, I can't bear to have them abandon me. They lull me to sleep with their gruesome news of the day. If I suddenly wake screaming from a nightmare, I look up and there's some guest pundit pontificating, reassuring me that everything is still in place. At eleven o'clock, the very habits I criticize in my daytime writing—the "normalization" of the Trump disaster, the repetitive questions, the fact that they can still smile and joke in this hell we have descended into—calms me.

It's just one of the many contradictions that comprise my relationship with television.

3 GROWING UP IN THE FIFTIES AND SIXTIES WITH TELEVISION

Television's Split Personality

From the beginning, TV has had a split personality. On the one hand, fifties television was full of fairy tales and fantasies meant solely to entertain and soothe—and encourage viewers to buy commodities to furnish idealized suburban lives. June Cleaver boosted both the industries in female glamour and Westinghouse appliances by cooking her pies (the best in the neighborhood of course—no Miss Minnie's in that white enclave) in pearls and heels. No one got cancer, Lassie always came home, and Father always knew best. We didn't know at the time that Robert Young (slightly later to become the first beloved TV doctor, Marcus Welby) actually struggled with alcoholism, that Ozzie was a domestic tyrant, and that his son Ricky, after a brief but dazzling career as a teen idol, would suffer from drug addiction and a marriage as far from the fictional Nelsons[1] as Lassie was from my own dog Dakota, who would just as soon wander into another county than come home when I call.

The most-watched hosts were relaxed, non-abrasive, good-humored: Hugh Downs, Arthur Godfrey, Garry Moore, Tennessee Ernie Ford, Dave Garroway (who in reality was sustained by daily doses of liquid cocaine, known in those days as "The Doctor"). Viewers trusted that contestants on *The $64,000 Question* and *Twenty-One*, sweating in their sound-proof booths, were really racking their brains to come up with the answers to the questions. For little kids, there was *Ding Dong School, Kukla, Fran and Ollie, Captain Kangaroo*

FIGURE 2 *The idealized fifties family watching a multi-function Motorola TV.* The Advertising Archives/Alamy.

FIGURE 3 *The Adventures of Ozzie and Harriet.* Shown: Ricky Nelson, Harriet Nelson, Ozzie Nelson, David Nelson. ABC/ Photofest.

and, a bit later, the ultimate soother, *Mr. Roberts*. On *Winky Dink* you could put a saran-wrap type film over the screen and "participate."

But TV discovered early on that it had tremendous power to disrupt the very fantasy world it created. Sometimes that disruption came in the fifties via gritty dramas, created by playwrights and directors, some of whom were to become famous in movies, known for their realism and willingness to tackle controversial issues from alcoholism and racism to conformism and McCarthyism: Elia Kazan, Delbert Mann, Arthur Penn, John Frankenheimer, Sidney Lumet, Reginald Rose (*Twelve Angry Men*); Paddy Chayefsky (*Marty*), Tad Mosel (*The Petrified Forest*), Rod Serling (*Requiem for a Heavyweight*). I, being a nerdy kid, loved the drama "playhouses," which were as formative of my intellectual and political thinking as anything I was reading.

But television wasn't only a showplace for fantasy sitcom or realistic drama. Until 1981, when George Bush's administration began censorship of media coverage of military operations, Americans got uncensored footage that undoubtedly played a large role in galvanizing the anti–Vietnam War movement: shocking scenes of napalmed children, decimated villages, footage of bodies being mangled by shrapnel. *New Yorker* TV critic Michael Arlen called Vietnam the "living room war" because it was "brought to the people predominantly by television"[2]—and, according to historian Charles Patch Jr., "showed the war as it was—a confused, fragmented, and questionable endeavor."[3] When Walter Cronkite, a month after the Tet Offensive, ended his broadcast with the recommendation that the United States find an honorable way out, "not as victors" but in recognition of stalemate, Lyndon Johnson told his press secretary that if he had lost Walter Cronkite, he had lost Mr. Average Citizen. A month later LBJ announced on prime-time television that he would not seek or accept the nomination for another term. It was "the first time in American history," writes David Halberstam, that "a war had been declared over by an anchorman."[4]

Television also played a huge role in raising national consciousness about racism. The Supreme Court, in 1954, ruled on *Brown v. Board of Education*, the collective name given to the five cases challenging and the constitutionality of separate but equal education, and integration was legally instituted. The ruling made a national hero out of Thurgood Marshall. But it wasn't until 1957 that a federal judge ordered the integration of Central High in Little Rock, Arkansas. And nine Black students—chosen among the best and brightest of

FIGURE 4 Walter Cronkite broadcasting from Vietnam, 1968. CPA Media Pte, Ltd./Alamy.

the middle-class Black community—prepared for their first day at school.

Orval Faubus, claiming it was for the protection of the nine students and the "tranquility" of the city, ordered the state's National Guard to block the students' entrance. The seventeen days of vicious bystander violence that followed were encouraged rather than quieted by the Guard. ("What are your orders?" someone asked one of the soldiers; "Keep the niggers out!" he answered.) When fifteen-year-old Elizabeth Eckford, who had inadvertently been left out of the protective phalanx of ministers organized to accompany the students, attempted to enter the school alone, a guard shoved his rifle in her face while the crowd terrified her with jeers: "Lynch her! Lynch her!"; "Go home, you bastard of a Black bitch!"; "No nigger bitch is going to get in our school!"[5]

This kind of behavior was probably not a huge surprise to locals. But this time, a junior reporter for NBC had been sent down to Little Rock to cover events. His name was John Chancellor, and he "watched in agony and captured it all for NBC." The murder of Emmett Till had brought the national press out, too, but they didn't come with cameras and film crews. Chancellor, under the direction of Reuven Frank, who understood the power of television, had been advised to "let the pictures do the talking."[6] And they did. Iconic scene: Elizabeth Eckford, looking down at the sidewalk, approaching the steps of Central High in Little Rock, Arkansas while white bigots, ugly with rage, shouted vile insults.

FIGURE 5 Elizabeth Eckford harassed by racists at Little Rock Central High, September 6, 1957. Everett Collection Historical/ Alamy.

The news was only twelve minutes long in 1957, but every night NBC led with Little Rock. Among racists, this earned NBC the title of "Nigger Broadcasting System."[7] But for those who were of a mind to be "woke," the coverage of Little Rock was galvanizing. Growing up in Newark, New Jersey, and ten years old when Central High was integrated, segregation had been something of an abstraction to me. Although there was plenty of racism exhibited by our parents and teachers in my inner-city, immigrant neighborhood, Blacks and whites were together in the classroom and on the athletic field. And I'd never witnessed any bigotry as blatantly violent as was exhibited by the mob at Central High. My grade-school teachers treated the Black kids in my class—especially the boys—differently. But I'd never even heard of lynching until Little Rock. (It was different for my daughter, who was given James Baldwin's *Going to Meet the Man* to read when she was 12, but that was in 2011.)

After the *Brown v. Board* ruling, newspapers and magazines hailed Thurgood Marshall as "Mr. Civil Rights," and he made the cover of *TIME* magazine. I had no awareness of the significance of any of it, however, until I saw those faces on TV, spitting poison at the Black teenager—not that much older than I but far more courageous than I imagined I could ever be—walking down the path to Little Rock's Central High. I wasn't alone. The brutal backlash that followed *Brown*, televised for the entire nation to see, helped turn a struggle seen by many Northerners as a "Southern thing" into a social movement.

When I teach the Civil Rights movement in my classes, I do it the way I learned about it myself. I work backward from those televised images, which still have the power to shock, to *Brown v. Board of Education*. The decision was a landmark not only in blasting apart *Plessy v. Ferguson* but in its innovative use of social science and psychology to

▶

demonstrate the pernicious effects of racism on the souls of both Black and white children. Other lawyers scoffed when Thurgood Marshall brought psychologist Kenneth Clark in to testify about his experiments with a pair of dolls, identical in every way except for color. Black and white school children had been asked a series of questions: which is the nice doll? Which is the bad doll? Which doll would you like to play with? The majority of Black children, Clark reported, attributed the positive characteristics to the white doll, the negative characteristics to the Black doll. When Clark asked one final question, "Which doll is like you?" the children looked at him, he says "as though he were the devil himself" for putting them in that predicament. Northern children often ran out of the room; southern children looked ashamed and embarrassed. Clark recalled one little boy who laughed, "Who am I like? That doll! It's a nigger and I'm a nigger!" It's a testimony that still has power, even in the twenty-first century, when I played video of it for a classroom of freshman in a course on social movements of the sixties.

Disney Made Me Diet

It's standard to fault the fashion industry—particularly the late sixties "British Invasion" of Twiggy, Mary Quant, and the sudden preference for lean, boyish female bodies for the beginnings of the obsession with dieting that ultimately led to an epidemic of eating disorders in the eighties and nineties.

I blame Walt Disney.

For before we became compulsive consumers of body-perfecting products and services, we first had to learn that the body *is* a commodity, capable of being shaped to resemble idealized images. And in my life as a female body, the Mouseketeers were a turning point.

It's true that I was particularly vulnerable. Until my younger sister was born, I was the baby of our family. Then, when I was four, she was brought into the house and I began to eat. First, I'm told (it may be a family myth), it was her toe, which they say I tried to bite off the first night she came home. Then it was chunks of white bread, gauged from the middle of the loaf, compressed into chewy lumps and dunked in mustard. I got fatter and fatter, and more and more afraid and ashamed of my body. I couldn't climb the ropes or jump over the horse in gym class, and the gym teacher shook his head scornfully and occasionally called me names. I dreaded going to school and many mornings, pretending sickness, I would hold the thermometer near the radiator. Once I went too far and it burst, causing shape-shifting droplets of mercury to spray all over the linoleum floor. They were fascinating to look at as they scurried this way and that, but I'd heard mercury was poisonous, so I had to call my mother in. She let me stay home anyway; suffering from depression herself, she couldn't deal with my sobbing when forced to go to school.

So: *The Mickey Mouse Club*, which premiered in 1955 when I was probably at the nadir of self-shame, found an especially ripe target in me. Does "target" seem excessively conspiratorial? The fact is that Walt very consciously set out to exploit the potential of baby boomers as consumers, as did all the kids' shows. They had a powerful sales tool: "Most of the children's-show hosts were hucksters in the guise of father figures. There was the friendly hunter (Buffalo Bill) or a friendly museum watchman (Captain Kangaroo) That combination of warmth and authority . . . was a powerhouse sales tool. If Dad says Wonder Bread is good for you, then it must be true."[8]

From the beginning, *The Mickey Mouse Club* was a bonanza for merchandisers.[9] The show featured more ads than any other at the time—twenty-two per episode. And Disney was (and "Disney, Inc." still is) a master at commodifying entertainment, from Davy Crockett hats and Spin and Marty books to tie-ins with Mattel toys. In 1955, when *Club* premiered, Mattel had annual sales of four million dollars. That Christmas, it began to advertise on *Mickey Mouse Club*; within a few years sales topped thirty-five million.

A huge source of revenue came from the promotion of mini-stars whose every fashion choice and hobby, featured on the pages of teen magazines, afforded opportunities to sell, sell, sell. At the beginning of each show, the chosen ones proudly introduced themselves: "Annette!" "Darlene!" "Cubby!" "Bobby!" Mouseketeer hats? If you were born in the years between 1946 and 1952 it's highly likely you had one. But the most enviable Mouseketeer for me—Annette Funicello—didn't just have a hat with ears and a cute little pleated skirt. She also had breasts—at first modest, but growing more prominent with every season, eliciting both adolescent lust and snickers from the boys and teaching

FIGURE 6 The Mickey Mouse Club. Shown from left: Jimmie Dodd, Annette Funicello, Tommy Cole, Doreen Tracey. Walt Disney Pictures/ABC/Photofest.

girls, as Susan Douglas remarks, that whether desired or demeaned, they were defined by their bodies.[10]

Fashion has always been a harsh dictator. But in previous twentieth-century periods, the dissemination of images was limited to high fashion magazines or, for those who couldn't afford Chanel, sketches in Sears Roebuck catalogues. The post-war period changed all that. There was a new consumer—eventually to be called baby boomers, first generation to constitute a distinctive "youth market"—and there were new media (teenage-geared movies, magazines, television shows) to pump up our desire, our desperation to look like the teen celebrities (and a little later on, the models) that seemed so perfect to us. Photo spreads designed specifically for teens now began to dictate our fantasies and expectations more than books. Goodbye Jo March, hello Gidget.

The most desirable teenage body in the early Sixties, when a return to domesticity was still winning out over the cool, androgynous look emerging from Carnaby Street, was a version of the hourglass. Annette had a tiny waist and perky breasts, as did Sandra Dee, as did Connie Stevens and teenage Elizabeth Taylor; it was a feature that was accentuated by the belted shirtwaist dresses favored in those days. I had the potential but was about twenty pounds overweight by the standards of those times, so the summer before high school I began the endless cycle of dieting—losing weight—gaining weight—dieting—gaining weight—that has been a constant in my life. After a summer of cottage cheese and hamburger patties without the bun, I started high school on the hottest day of the year in a tightly belted form-fitting burnt-sienna-colored wool dress that I had chosen for the reveal and wasn't going to give up no matter how scratchy it felt.

For a while, I looked "right." Unfortunately for me, by the time I was a junior in high school, being small breasted and long limbed was in style. While I could approximate the curvy idea of the fifties through diet and the right kind of bra, my 5-foot 2-inch, big-booty body—shaped by centuries of Eastern European genes—made it impossible for me to look anything like a Twiggy, or even a Peggy Lipton of *The Mod Squad*. To add insult to injury, my bust—the one feature of my body that had satisfied the "mammary madness" of the 1950s—was now not just out of fashion, but an embarrassing signifier of an out-of-date ideal of femininity. The hourglass figure had been valued as the symbolic embodiment of a domestic (male-sexualized, reproductive) destiny. The flat-chested, lanky look, in contrast, made you a cool girl who had the sexual ease and the social freedom that I craved. As for my big booty, I was too old to personally benefit, but not too old to appreciate it when hip-hop took its revenge.

It took decades of escalating eating disorders before fashion designers and magazines were willing to acknowledge the role of idealized imagery associating slimness with glamour, modernity, and freedom; ultimately, they did come around. But it took more

▶

than feminist analysis to do it: it took empirical studies demonstrating that as Western ideals spread across the globe, so did eating problems. An influential study was that of anthropologist Anne Becker. Because of their remote location, the Fiji Islands hadn't access to television until 1995 when a single station, broadcasting programs from the US, Great Britain, and Australia was introduced. Until that time, Fiji had no reported cases of eating disorders, and a study conducted by Becker showed that most Fijian girls and women, no matter how large, were comfortable with their bodies. In 1998, just three years after the station began broadcasting, 11 percent of girls reported vomiting to control weight, and 62 percent reported dieting during the previous months. Becker was stunned. She thought local custom would withstand the influence of Western media. She hadn't yet understood that we live in an empire of images, and that there are no protective borders.

The Suburban TV Family and Its Shadow

"America is the impression I get from looking in the television set,"

ALLEN GINSBERG, 1956

Robert Young, who played Jim Anderson, the father who knew best in the popular series that ran from 1954 to 1960, was often asked by strangers for advice about social conduct and raising a family. They didn't ask Jane Wyatt, who played Margaret Anderson or Barbara Billingsley, who played mom on *Leave It to Beaver*. Mothers were not supposed to be wise; they were supposed to be warm and supportive. Most of the cast members knew this was far from the way things actually were. Young recalls: "Originally the show was supposed to be called '*Father Knows Best?*'" The question mark made the phrase a jab at Father, "who always assumed he is head of the household, but everybody knows that Mother really is." But the sponsor, Kent cigarettes, objected. It wasn't just a suggestion; as Young relates it, "the deal rested on that one question mark coming off."[11]

More than just the question mark or gender roles was at issue; as writer Mel Diamond put it "As a writer, if you had experience and balls, you got neutered very fast."[12] When Billy Gray (who played son Bud) suggested more realistic teen vernacular ("crazy, man" was happening then, he recalls) he was told no, that "it would offend people." And when Scott paper became the new sponsor, they weren't permitted to show their toilet paper (if they did, Billy remarks, "it would suggest people had assholes"). Of course, there were no Blacks or Jews on the show, and the Latino gardener on *Father Knows* was improbably named Frank Smith. "We were supposed to be in a small town" is Jane Wyatt's explanation, and adds, somewhat defensively, "There were places like that."

But Billy Gray rejects that explanation, pointing out that the show ran concurrent with the Civil Rights movement. "It was if we were in a vacuum or some kind of enchanted forest. It wasn't taking into account the reality of the world. It was just an advertiser's vision of what the world should be."[13]

Barbara Billingsley had no problem with the disinfected world of *Leave It to Beaver* or her role in it. While she admits that she was portrayed as though she "had no brains," it "seemed to be a normal family to me. It didn't seem unusual that the woman would be serving breakfast and be there when the kids came back from school. Sure there were a lot of working women, but nothing like today. Being in a dress all the time was the producer's idea. They always wanted us to be the ideal, which meant I had to be dressed, no curlers." And of course there were the pearls, which actually were chosen for pragmatic reasons (Billingsley had a hollow in her neck that created a shadow, and the pearls covered it) but for feminists became a symbol of how far-fetched that ideal of mom was.[14]

These shows certainly didn't mirror my own reality. Until I was about to enter high school, we lived above a butcher shop in what would become known as the inner city of Newark, New Jersey. I passed two bars on my walk to school and the most green I got to see was at "the track," where my sister and I scoured the grounds for winning but carelessly discarded place and show tickets. On Halloween, my parent sent us out in the dark alone, oblivious to whether we got our candy from the neighborhood bars or not. They were more afraid of us catching our "death of cold" than they were of other people doing anything bad to us. When I was a preteen, we moved to the Weequahic section, immortalized by Philip Roth. There, the houses actually had lawns and there was a huge park down in the fancy end of the neighborhood, where the families of doctors and lawyers lived (and where a cop once told me and my Black male friend to "get gone."). Still, it was nothing like the suburbs, where some of my wealthier friends were moving, in white flight from the increasing racial diversity of the neighborhood.

It's a fascinating but little discussed fact that the producers who sold the WASP-y suburban vision of American life were themselves Jewish. Yes, the trouble-free, all-white, Christian world of fifties television was largely the product of immigrants like my own family who created that world from their own fantasies of what it meant to be American, their fears of repelling Christian viewers and/or their ambivalence about reinforcing Jewish stereotypes. Jews were prominent behind the scenes: up until the mid-1980s, ABC, NBC, and CBS were Jewish owned (Leonard Goldenson, David Sarnoff, William Paley, respectively).[15] But from 1954 to 1972 there wasn't one prime-time show featuring a leading character who was Jewish. (The one fifties show featuring a Jewish family—*The Goldbergs*—was cancelled in 1954, after battling for five years against the perception that it was "too Jewish.")[16]

Eventually, in the 1970s, television's representation of the family was to become more diverse. That meant the gentile leads could have Jewish buddies like Rhoda Morgenstern, and family-oriented sitcoms were either ostentatiously ethnic or working class. (*All in the Family*, *Roseanne*, and a host of Black family sitcoms located in the ghetto.) Suburban family life mostly remained the subject of gentle nostalgia in shows like *Happy Days* and *The Wonder Years*. Arguably even *The Cosby Show*, which broke important ground by depicting an upper middle-class professional Black family who lived in a brownstone and did *not* suffer poverty, reproduced many of the same myths of the fifties family sitcoms precisely by showing that a Black family could be "just like any other American family." That is: *happy* with things as they were.

So: When I saw the first episode of Matthew Weiner's *Mad Men*, I could barely contain my excitement. It was the first time television was presenting what I had experienced as the reality of the post-War period: work-obsessed father away much of the time; depressed mother; racism and anti-Semitism depicted rather than stuffed away in the closet. And most of all, the multitude of ways, both minor and major, that men treated women (as voluptuous office manager Joan Holloway, played by Christina Henricks, puts it) like "something between a mother and a waitress, and . . ." She doesn't specify a word but it's clear: sex toy. Or perhaps, whore.

No, *Mad Men* does not take place in the kind of neighborhoods I grew up in. The genius of *Mad Men* was not to move the nuclear family to someplace more like Newark, New Jersey, but to flay open the idealized surface of the suburban world of *Father Knows Best* and *Leave It to Beaver*. From the first episode, we are introduced to a corporate culture that is casually racist, anti-Semitic, and gender hierarchical. At home in the suburbs, Betty Draper (January Jones) dresses much like June Cleaver (except at night, when she wears lingerie we'd never have seen June in) and has the same finishing-school manners. But in the second episode she experiences a loss of feeling in her hands that sends her to a psychiatrist, who does nothing but sit and smoke, listen to her ramble, and then reports to husband Don (Jon Hamm) on how seriously disturbed she is. Don doesn't hang around the kitchen the way the fifties sitcom dads did—he's head of the creative department of an ad agency and spends much of his time at the office. But he has mistresses—and dark secrets, both from his past and in his present.

As we will eventually find out, Don is hardly fully evolved, but the men he works with haven't even left the cave. They spend much of their time hanging out together like frat boys, laughing at each other's offensive jokes and discussing how they'd like to get under the dress of "new girl" Peggy Olsen (Elisabeth Moss). ("To you, the whole world is like one big brassiere strap waiting to be snapped," Don tells Pete Campbell, one of the most shamelessly sexist.) The women appear to expect and welcome what would come to be known as "being objectified," seeing it as the route to snagging a husband and house in the suburbs. Joan, giving Peggy a tour of the department, advises her to make the most of her "darling ankles" and Nanette of the switchboard pool also comments on Peggy's legs, adding that "Bet Mr. Draper would like them if he could see them." As Peggy is taken from office to office by Joan, she gets the same advice from men and women alike: make the most of your physical assets, sweetie, and don't be afraid to show that body off. Joan tells her that when she gets home she should get naked, put a bag over her head and assess her flaws in her mirror at home. She also recommends a gynecologist, who gives Peggy Enovid but instructs her not to become a "strumpet" to justify the expense. (His cheery condescension—"Scooch down the table, sweetheart"—sends a special kind of chill in 2020, as "Peggy" has gone on to star in *The Handmaid's Tale*.) Later that night Peggy has sex with a very drunk Pete (Vincent Kartheiser) who's been celebrating his last night as a "free man."[17]

When *Mad Men* first aired, some critics complained that the sexism was overdone. And it's true that there's barely a scene that doesn't show men behaving in an entitled, crude way with the women who work in the office. For me, though, and in contrast to the familiar nostalgia for the period (the first season takes place in 1960) the show "got it"—all of it, including the over-the-top sexism and the seeming obedience, even collusion, of the women. Like the women in *Mad Men*, I craved being the object of male attention, and was willing to overlook what today would be defined as abusive. Far from complaining, I looked for ways to impress my male teachers and the boys at the same time: sarcasm, cynicism, and lots of dirty talk. I also pretty much let the boys I had crushes on do whatever they wanted with me, short of actual intercourse, and whether or not I was enjoying myself. Most of the time I wasn't.

As for the seemingly more serious, responsible Don Draper, who looks like an urbane Marlboro Man, he isn't interested in going to a strip club with the boys the night of Pete's bachelor party, and takes Peggy's hand off his own when she (understandably) gets the idea it's what bosses want; for much of the episode we are led to believe he is different. When he stays overnight in the city with Midge (Rosemarie DeWitt), the woman who is his artsy, freedom-loving "medicine" (as she describes herself) and says "I wish you would marry me," we assume he's single, and she is setting the rules. Um . . . not exactly. At the very end of the first episode we see him get off a commuter train, walk down a suburban street, open the door to a pretty but modest home that could be a set for *Father Knows Best* and go upstairs to say goodnight to—surprise!—his wife. She's very blonde, very Breck girl, and she's clearly very used to never complaining when her husband stays late (or overnight) in the city. There are also two children.

The first scene of the episode had shown Don in a restaurant, trying to dream up an approach for Lucky Strike that will distract smokers from the studies that had been linking smoking to cancer. (The surgeon general's report will come out in 1964, but *Reader's Digest* was already making people nervous.) In the background, "Band of Gold" (referring to a wedding ring) is playing, but the episode is called "Smoke Gets in Your Eyes." (By the last episode of first the season, the music accompanying the ending credits will be Bob Dylan singing "The Times They Are a' Changing.")

Goodbye, June and Ward Cleaver and their perfect marriage. And as they exit, they take the nostalgia that suffused all previous shows about the fifties with them.

WHY THERE'S NO SPORTS IN THIS BOOK

Every book on the history of television has a chapter (or more) on sports. Mine doesn't. The reason is simple: I can't watch a sports event without smelling my father's cigar.

I don't mean remembering; I mean smelling. Acrid, soggy chewed end in a large glass ashtray, my father's cigars live in the DNA of my senses, ready to assault me with nausea at the mere sound of cheering fans at a football game.

My husband, who doesn't smoke, is only allowed to watch sports when I'm not in the room. I am a tyrant about this and feel absolutely justified in bossing him around.

"Do we have to have that on?"

"I thought you were working."

"Well I'm here now."

He's happy to change the channel, but it's too late. It's an afront to me that I had to endure even two minutes of it, and my mind is already counting all the injustices I've suffered at the hands of men who were oblivious to my needs.

▶

"And when are you going to empty the dishwasher? Or is that always my job?"

"Hey, I said I'd change the channel."

"Oh, forget it. I'll just go back in my office. It's the only place around here that isn't cluttered with your junk anyway."

My husband has every right to feel abused. He's nothing like my father. But he didn't grow up with him either. And just as he doesn't smell his cigar smoke, he doesn't see the nervous woman on the couch, silently smoking Kents. She has red hair, like me. She doesn't know how to drive a car, and she will never live in a home like Betty Draper's. My father doesn't see any need to save for a house. He's a travelling salesman on the road most of the time. The apartment they live in, near the airport, is ugly and isolated, and far from her old friends in the Weequahic section and relatives in Brooklyn. She is rarely allowed to visit them because my father doesn't like my mother's relatives, he considers them peasants.

As a child, I was scared of school, for a hundred different reasons, and staying home with my mother and the soaps was a refuge that lasted for me into adulthood. In my memory, it's always raining outside and that makes it feel okay to be at home. Sunny days remind me of my difference from the regular kids, who'd be playing sports

▶

while I read a book. Here, in the cave of our living room, the familiar characters on the soaps root me in a sense of normalcy, continuity and community. Odd, isn't it, that an unreal world would make me feel solid and safe? Or maybe not so odd, when you think of the thousands of *Fox and Friends* viewers—including Donald Trump—who, every day, are comforted by lies.

So when I broke down after my first marriage, I went home—to my mother and to the television. We spent our days depressed together, chain-smoking Kents and watching *General Hospital* on what passed in those days as a color set. I don't think this is actually the case, but in my memory I'm curled up against her. Her plump body is warm and although I know she is worried about me and my fast-dissolving marriage, I feel she is glad to have me there, sharing the trials and tribulations of Luke, Laura and the rest. Port Charles was so welcoming to us, anxiety-ridden in this barren New Jersey highway land. Unlike our actual neighbors in Fords, we knew everyone who lived in Port Charles, and they were always there, day after day. They were our community. And not just ours: the 1981 wedding of Laura and Luke (her former rapist!) drew thirty million viewers.

My father's big chair is empty—he's on the road—and the smell of cigarette smoke now rules the house.

4 THE EROSION OF THE FACT-BASED UNIVERSE

Daniel Boorstin's Prescient Insight

"Great unforeseen changes—the great forward strides of American civilization—have blurred the edges of reality. The pseudo-events which flood our consciousness are neither true nor false in the old familiar senses. The very same advances which have made them possible have also made the images— however planned, contrived, or distorted—more vivid, more attractive, and more persuasive than reality itself.

We cannot say that we are being fooled. It is not entirely inaccurate to say that we are being 'informed.' This world of ambiguity is created by those who believe they are instructing us, by our best public servants, and with our own collaboration. Our problem is the harder to solve because it is created by people working honestly and industriously at respectable jobs. It is not created by demagogues or crooks, by conspiracy or evil purpose. The efficient mass production of pseudo-events—in all kinds of packages, in black-and-white, in technicolor, in words, and in a thousand other forms—is the work of the whole machinery of our society. It is the daily product of men of good will. The media must be fed! The public must be informed! . . .

The American citizen thus lives in a world where fantasy is more real than reality, where the image has more dignity than its original."

DANIEL BOORSTIN, *The Image*, 1961[1]

James Brooks's 1987 film *Broadcast News*, with Holly Hunter and William Hurt, posed an ethical dilemma. Attractive, good-natured, and morally flexible anchorman Tom (Hurt), filming an interview with a survivor of date rape, tears up as she tells her story. The entire crew realizes it's a powerful moment; the problem is, the interview was shot with only one camera, and when Tom's eyes filled with tears, the camera was pointed at the woman telling her story. After a moment of disappointment, Tom comes up with a solution: he can bring himself to tears again and they can film it this time. Nothing wrong with that, right? It's not as though his reaction was a fiction. "After all, I did it the first time," Tom reassures the crew. But old-school journalist Jane (Hunter), when she finds out, doesn't see it that way. In fact, she's outraged, calls his action "god-damn awful," and breaks up with Tom over his breach with broadcast ethics. In faking tears—even though it replicated what actually had happened—"You crossed the line," she tells Tom. Tom's reply is probably the most trenchant point in the movie: "The line? They keep moving the little sucker all the time."

My students, proving Tom's point, found Jane's actions ridiculous. Here was this handsome hunk, offering a trip to Hawaii during which they could have fun sex, drink tropical drinks, and argue the respective merits of their positions, and Jane was turning him down? Over faking some tears? What was the big deal?

We had that discussion in 2005. By then, the idea that Tom's actions were morally questionable was a quaint—and quite boring—relic to my students. They had just watched a clip of Anderson Cooper, wandering through the rubble of Hurricane Katrina, picking through people's scattered belongings. We see his anguish mount as he picks up personal items and children's toys. He begins to choke up. He gestures to the cameraman to stop shooting. It's a version of the Tom moment, and none of my students found anything wrong with it. At first, they couldn't even see the comparison. True, Cooper isn't faking emotion. But the segment is taped, not live. If Cooper really wanted the eye of the camera to back off, I asked my students, why didn't he just edit the moment out? The answer is obvious: Anderson's distress made the story more human, more moving, more compelling television. (And showed off Cooper's modesty and integrity as well.)

In 2005, of course, no one at CNN was arguing with him about the ethics of exploiting his emotional reaction to concoct what Daniel Boorstin, with great prescience in 1961 called the "pseudo-event": reality configured and packaged for the viewer. Neither "true nor false in the old familiar sense," the pseudo-event is reality transformed into a contrived image with is "more vivid, more attractive, more impressive, and more persuasive than reality itself."

In 1961 Boorstin seemed alarmist. In 2020, the pseudo-event is the coin of the realm, but with a difference: the "old familiar" distinction between "true and false" is not just something that is occasionally straddled or stretched; it's become a distinction that is ignored, sometimes even flaunted. At one time, we were shocked to learn how much digital alteration goes into the creation of magazine imagery. By 2009, Adobe Photoshop had begun to market its digital software with the incitement to "Spread Lies" (remove those wrinkles, love handles, dog drool) in your photos. In 2020, 12-year-olds post glamour shots on Instagram as artfully retouched and transforming as the covers of *Vogue*.

It's important to distinguish the "pseudo" from the "fake." When Donald Trump accuses the liberal press of disseminating "fake news," he means that they are lying, making things up out of whole cloth (just because they hate him, he tells the public). The "pseudo," however, isn't exactly a lie, but occupies that territory Boorstin describes, which allows for entertaining "enhancement" to dominate over the bare simplicity of fact. It's a kind of retouching. But it's not just bodies that we retouch. The genre of historical fiction has been "pseudo"-factual for some time, but formerly, it had the saving grace of being recognized as such. We knew that Truman Capote's *In Cold Blood* was a special genre that combined fact and imagination. Over the past few decades, however, the distinction between what happened and what some writer creatively imagines as having happened has been challenged, first by historical fiction writers (such as Philippa Gregory) who claim impeccable factual status for their inventions, and then, even more profoundly, by films and television series that present their invented narratives via vivid, detailed, historically accurate costuming, sets, and digital magic of various sorts that scream "reality" to the viewer.

This kind of verisimilitude may seem innocuous. And certainly, it's visually entertaining, sometimes even dazzling. But it does make it very difficult to teach the ancient art of distinguishing reality from illusion, fact from fiction. Over the past ten to fifteen years, history—both ancient and recent—has become a treasure trove of narratives to be plundered for television series. Cable television, in particular, is loaded, from *Rome* through *The Tudors*, *Versailles*, *The Medicis*, *Reign*, *The Borgias* to *Victoria* and *The Crown*. And of course, all of Philippa Gregory. There are vast differences in the degree of accuracy and integrity these series bring to the screen. And really, I'd have no problem with any of them if little fact-checking boxes were to flash on the screen anytime one goes horribly astray. OK, so maybe that's too much to expect. But Keisha Hatchett in *TV Guide* goes over the other edge and suggests that while learning history in school "is fine if you're into that sort of thing," filling "your head with the knowledge of important events of yesterday through the stylish and fictionalized accounts of TV's hottest scripted shows" will do in a pinch: "While historical dramas might not be super accurate—hey, at least *The Tudors* covered the basics in between those steamy love scenes—they make history exciting with high-stakes drama and opulent costumes that are most certainly way out of your budget. If you're among those who can't get enough of these racy period pieces, grab a cup of tea and settle in."[2]

I love period dramas. I also like tea. Settling in to binge on a good series is my idea of paradise. But I also am an old-fashioned type who was sometimes actually interested in learning stuff at school, and it's my long-standing habit to fact-check whatever smells fishy to me. In my experience as a teacher, fewer and fewer students have that habit. I've had students argue with me about Anne Boleyn's life and death on the basis of Philippa Gregory's *The Other Boleyn Girl*—even worse, on the basis of the film, which takes even greater liberties with the facts. No, Anne Boleyn never was raped by Henry VIII, nor did she attempt to seduce her brother. But the gardens around the castles look so real in *The Other Boleyn Girl*, and Natalie Portman curtsies with such historical accuracy! How can a teacher challenge all that vibrantly simulated reality with boring old documents written in an outmoded English?

Fox and the Ascendancy of "Story" over Fact

Most of us know that Peggy Noonan wrote Ronald Reagan's speeches. But before there was Noonan, there was Roger Ailes, the founder and guiding light of Fox News. Ailes, then a freelance consultant, was called in to coach Ronald Reagan before his second debate with Walter Mondale. The Republican Party thinks of Reagan as The Great Communicator now, but the first debate had been a disaster: Reagan seemed tired and confused, and there was anxiety among his team that his age was becoming an obstacle. Against all advice, Ailes urged Reagan to go right for it rather than avoid it. And so a line that may well have won Reagan the presidency was prepared: ". . . and I want you to know that I will not make an age an issue in this campaign. I am not going to exploit for political purposes my opponent's youth and experience." It was probably Ailes's most successful application of his philosophy of television to politics: people don't want to be talked down to by politicians or newscasters. Rather, they want "to be made comfortable in every communications situation . . . So when you and I communicate, we are unconsciously judged by our audience against the standards set by Johnny Carson and Dan Rather . . . relaxed, informal, crisp, and entertaining."[3]

This became Reagan's signature style, and it had nothing to do with expertise, experience, intelligence, or ability to solve problems; he was our first TV-trained POTUS, and knew how to make viewers feel comfortable. And while Trump might scoff at feel-good liberals, the fact is that he too is a master at making his base feel good, as Reagan was before him. And it was the secret of Fox News, too: not the ideology, but the creation of comfort and warm, listened-to feelings among those huge audiences alienated by the coastal elitism of stations like MSNBC, which Roger Ailes rightly discerned "left a lot of America on the outside."[4] Taking advantage of an already existing duality in values and deliberately appealing to those who felt dismissed or looked down on, Fox ultimately widened the chasm that characterizes what pundits now refer to, casually, as our polarized political culture.

Fox also changed—for the entire cable news world, not just the crowd that frequented Sean Hannity—what was permissible, what was familiar, what kept people from changing the channel, riveted to sensational breaking news, outsize personalities, the excitement of politics as horse race, the "optics" of gaffes and everything else that makes me despair of what TV news has become. Previously, the news came to us via fatherly, trusted newscasters like Walter Cronkite who stayed as faithful as possible to the ideal of the "news that's fit to print": non-sensationalizing, non-dramatizing, and as grounded in established fact as possible. By the time of Bill Clinton's troubles, tabloid news had begun encroaching into liberal broadcasting now feeling the need to compete with Fox. It hardly seems startling nowadays, but it was unprecedented in 1992 when CNN broadcast live

Gennifer Flowers's press conference detailing her affair with Clinton.

Fox also helped change the rules about the factual as well as the "fit." In 1975, Bruce Herschensohn, former Nixon aide, had impressed Roger Ailes enormously with a memo of a "tactical programming proposal" to TVN, the forerunner to Fox News. It highlights, without shame or qualm, techniques of manipulating an audience; they include: "Catch phrases . . . which seem to be factual though they are, in fact, editorializations"; "repetition," which creates a news event through repeated assertion. "The creation of the most important story today," Herschensohn wrote, "becomes the most important story a week from today" through repetition; it's "the oldest and most effective propaganda technique."[5] Sound familiar? Or is "No Collusion, No Obstruction" enough to convey the idea?

It was a marriage made in heaven (hell?) when Trump and Roger Ailes got together. However, Trump, as a salesman and self-promoter, didn't need Ailes to teach him how to make a lie pass itself off as fact. His version—called "truthful hyperbole"—was just less transparent (and seemingly more innocuous) than Kellyanne's [Kellyanne Conway, Counselor to the President]—probably because it was drawn from the world of the ad rather than the news. Advertisements, unlike journalism, have always fudged the

▶

line between fact and consumer seduction—and in *The Art of the Deal*, Trump conceptualizes it:

> . . . *I play to people's fantasies. People may not always think big themselves, but they can still get very excited by those who do. That's why a little hyperbole never hurts. People want to believe that something is the biggest and the greatest and the most spectacular.*
>
> *I call it truthful hyperbole. It's an innocent form of exaggeration—and a very effective form of promotion.*[6]

The example Trump gives in the book is referring to himself as "Brooklyn's Largest Builder." And it may be possible that at the beginning, he truly saw no difference between the "innocence" of pumping up one's image to sell a construction job and doctoring photos of his inaugural crowds. Perhaps he hasn't always been a bald-faced liar but truly imagined that becoming POTUS was only different in degree from being a salesman. Maybe from "Brooklyn's Largest Builder" to "The Greatest President the US Has Ever Known" was a slippery slope that he tumbled down without full awareness. Maybe lying is a habit so ingrained in Trump—inhaled and ingested from his father, Roy Cohn, and others—that he truly doesn't know the difference between fact and fiction.

Actually, "No Collusion, No Obstruction" is worse than an editorialization in drag. It's factually false that Robert Mueller found Trump innocent of obstruction. Compare it, for example, to the Fox creation of "The War on Christmas." The phrase is dripping with disdain for liberals obsessed with diversity, is implicitly Christian-centric, and may be seen as covertly anti-Semitic as well. But although some people may have felt their traditions were being attacked, there certainly wasn't an orchestrated plot to abolish Christmas. That Mueller concluded "No obstruction" is false no matter how one feels. The spinning of out-and-out lies into "possibilities" or "interpretations" or "perspectives" is what Kellyanne Conway tried to do when she described Trump's gross exaggeration of the size of his inauguration an "alternative fact."[7] The word "fact," however, exposed the duplicity. No one had ever put the words "alternative" and "fact" together before, not publicly anyway—as a fact was supposed to be a fact, period, not a "version" among others.

But the blame isn't to be placed only on Fox. Culturally, we had been moving toward alternative realities for some time before Fox made it official protocol.

O. J. and DNA

In the spring of 1995, before the O. J. Simpson verdict, I asked my undergraduate students what they thought about Simpson's guilt or innocent. "Oh, he's innocent!" said one (who happened to be a young white man). "On what basis have you come to that conclusion?" I asked. "Well . . . I don't know . . . he's a football hero, and handsome, and seems nice and friendly, and, well . . . I just sort of see it that way." When I pressed him further he just kept repeating: "I just sort of see it that way."

"I just sorta see it that way": that argument was many of the jurists' justifications for their verdicts, too. Detective Philip Vannater, one explained, didn't look jurors in the eyes and thus couldn't be trusted. But criminologist Henry Lee's warm smile ("Henry Lee was just so likeable") made him a thoroughly dependable witness. But the most anti-fact, pro-"just sorta seeing it" explanation of all was offered when one of the jurors, questioned after the verdict about the DNA evidence, shrugged it off: "To me, the DNA was just a long string of numbers . . . it was just a waste of time. It was way out there and carried absolutely no weight with me."[8] DNA as something one could accept or reject? By 2020, the dismissal of science via climate-change deniers and creationists may be familiar stuff. In 1994, however, it was shocking to me.

The Simpson trial, in my personal history of watershed moments of television's contribution to the decline of fact, is way up there. I watched it all. My husband and I had just moved to Kentucky, our new home was in the country, and initially we only had a few channels, one of which was Court Television (Court TV), which had launched in 1991. We became addicted, mesmerized by how defense lawyers, aided and abetted by the sympathies and susceptibilities of jurors, were able to construct an alternative reality to counter the massive factual evidence that Simpson killed Nicole and Ron Goldman.

Perhaps there was nothing especially new there in terms of lawyerly strategy. But televised gavel to gavel, it became available for all to see. (Court TV presented seven hundred hours; CNN six hundred. When the verdict was announced on October 3, 1995, it was covered live on every major network and drew an estimated 150 million viewers.) The lawyers themselves were open about what they were doing. Simpson defense lawyer Barry Scheck, for example: "What people really do," he told Lawrence Schiller, "is listen to testimony and turn it into a story that makes sense to them . . . the key is to get the jurors to integrate all the information into your story line." As the defense team planned their strategy, Scheck wrote on a blackboard the story that he believed would be most compelling: "Integrity of the Evidence: Contaminated, Compromised and Corrupted."[9] Once that story was made real for the jurors, it would make little difference that even if one threw out all the evidence that defense claimed was contaminated and compromised, one would still be left with more than enough evidence to convict Simpson. The narrative, repeated over and over, won the day and relieved jurors of the responsibility to actually go through the evidence, sifting and weighing the relative strengths of each piece.

Duct Tape under the Bed

The ascendancy of the compelling story over factually established evidence has been the trajectory of much broadcast (and print) journalism, too. Steven Stark, in *Glued to the Set*, sees the emergence of "magazine" shows like *60 Minutes* (1968, CBS) as crucial in changing the nature of news broadcasting. Producer Don Hewitt's big insight: people were less likely to change the channel if the news was as appealing as *Kojak* and other fictions that had the look and detail of reality but with interesting plots and characters to whom viewers could become attached. The goal, as Stark puts it, was to "package reality as well as Hollywood packages fiction." The danger: Packaging reality requires the stitching together of facts into narrative. And while this is something we do to some degree anytime we construct a sentence, to compete with Hollywood the narratives of the news had to be entertaining as well as informative. A little creativity—sometimes more than a little creativity—was useful. And "breaking news"—even if not yet verified—was a great protection against things drying up. The result, according to Stark, was a "thinner line between fact and rumor."[10]

Actually, when "the story" is your standard, it's not just that fact becomes compromised. "Reality" also becomes created. Those stories that are highlighted and repeated (as they tend to be, given the challenge of filling up the 24-hour news cycle) are likely to segue into the category of fact, while those that are ignored slip into the purgatory of inattention—

unless some freshly exciting breaking news intervenes. True, if the story is ultimately proved groundless—as frequently happens—retractions may be announced—but buried on page 10 and probably not even mentioned on television.

A classic example is the Richard Jewell case. Jewell was the security guard who found three pipe bombs in a backpack planted July 27 at the 1996 Olympics in Atlanta. Jewell alerted the police and the park was evacuated. Early news reports celebrated Jewell as a hero, but within three days the media had begun portraying him as a possible suspect, for no apparent reason other than their own theory that Jewell had planted the bomb in order to find it and become a hero. The FBI searched his home, maintained 24-hour surveillance on him, and investigated his background. Although he passed a polygraph, Jewell was now headlined as "The Hero Turned Suspect" who fit the "criminal profile" of a "lone bomber," a frustrated police "wannabe," and—the coup de grâce—with duct tape under his bed and curtains drawn in his house.[11]

"The Hero Turned Suspect" was all we read about, all we heard about for weeks. (Tom Brokaw: "The speculation is that the FBI is close to making the case. They probably have enough to arrest him right now, probably enough to prosecute him, but you always want to have enough to convict him as well. There are still some holes in the case."[12]) "Holes" was an understatement, as no real evidence against Jewell existed, and the bomber was ultimately found to be Eric Robert Rudolph, who would later bomb a lesbian nightclub and two abortion clinics.[13] Jewell was formally cleared in October, but by then the media story—so coherent and convincing (The darkened house! The duct tape!)—had become the more dominant reality than the facts. Many people today still think he was the bomber.

Lawlessness in the Superdome

Some of the biggest stories of our times have perpetuated unexamined racist, classist, and gender conceptions. In 2005, Hurricane Katrina ravaged New Orleans—and media coverage confirmed every racist and classist assumption about the poor people forced to take refuge in the Superdome. Mayor Ray Nagin appeared on *Oprah Winfrey* and described being "in that frigging Superdome for five days watching dead bodies, watching hooligans killing people, raping people" On the same show, Police Chief Eddie Compass reported that "little babies were getting raped" at the Superdome. The headlines and tickers proclaimed "Complete lawlessness," "People shooting at police officers," "Growing gangs roaming the devastated area," "People stealing TV sets and microwaves," "Sniper attacks by roving gangs."[14]

Of course, there were also the heroes: "Reporters risk their lives to get the story." Jeanne Meserve: "It was a heroic piece of work by CNN employees . . . Big words of praise for them and for Mark Biello, who went out and ended up in that water, trying to get the rescue boats over partially submerged railroad tracks." Aaron Brown: "Our thanks to you [Jean Meserve] for your efforts. It—you don't need to hear this from me but you know, sometimes people think that we're a bunch of kind of wacky thrill seekers doing this work, sometimes, and no one who has listened to the words you've spoken or the tone of your voice could possibly think that now."[15]

When the facts emerged, it was established that of the 841 deaths related to the storm, only four were identified as gunshot victims. And National Guard spokesman Major Ed Bush, who was inside the Superdome the whole time, was aghast at the jungle stories: "What I saw was just tremendous amounts of people helping people." He noted that most of those revelations, which also just happened to give the lie to stereotypes about poor African Americans, never made it on TV or into the newspapers.[16]

Hillary's Pneumonia

Arguably the most famous victim of runaway media story telling is Hillary Clinton. Consider, for example, "Hillary's Health Scare." In September 2016, the then-Democratic candidate for the presidency had pneumonia and, like many women, had carried on despite her doctor's advice.[17] She insisted on attending a 9/11 commemorative ceremony, and nearly fainted—something that has happened to others standing in the sun at long political events. Then, she committed the unpardonable sin of disappearing from the media's sight for ninety minutes while she sought calm and cool—and water—in her daughter Chelsea's apartment.

The media immediately issued a missing persons alert. Where was she? Where did she go? When a video surfaced showing her unsteadily entering her van, supported by the Secret Service, and the news of her pneumonia was released, reporters were convinced she had been deliberately concealing her illness, revealing it only when she was caught in the act of fainting. When she emerged from Chelsea's apartment she seemed smiling and well—another cause for suspicion. Was it really pneumonia? And if so, why hadn't she told the press about it? Hillary's explanation was that she didn't announce her illness because she thought she could just push on through, no big deal. And as it turned out, John Kerry and others had also suffered pneumonia without announcing it to the world. But that wouldn't have made much of a story, and "Secretive Hillary," "Untrustworthy Hillary" did. The mainstream media played and replayed the visual of her knees buckling and adored posing the unanswered questions that remained concerning Hillary's health scare. NBC News:

"Clinton's campaign has been tight-lipped about the Sunday incident, releasing only two short statements throughout the day. Many lingering questions could be easily cleared up by the campaign, while others will take time."

First among the questions: "Why hide the pneumonia diagnosis?":

She received her pneumonia diagnosis on Friday, but the public was not told about it until hours after the incident at the memorial, raising questions about whether Clinton had any plans to ever inform the public . . . Opponents are already seeing the incident as proof of their claims that Clinton has been hiding health issues. And others may now be more incredulous of the campaign's statements on her health . . .[18]

The notion that Clinton was covering up more serious health issues was a favorite among more right-wing sources. "Why was an email sent to Mrs. Clinton from a top aide about a drug used to treat symptoms of Parkinson's disease?" ominously queried Cliff Kincaid. Parkinson's disease was just one of many disorders Clinton was suspected of hiding—even before her pneumonia: descriptions of her as "exhausted" (or without "stamina," as Trump was fond of putting it) and unable to stand up on her own; suggestions of "traumatic brain injury" and talk of "seizures" and "dysphasia"; demands for fuller health records from Clinton—all while Trump produced a laughable doctor's letter describing his health in such rigorous medical language as "astonishingly excellent" and declaring that he would be "the healthiest individual ever elected to the presidency."[19]

Hillary's health scare amounted to nothing. It acquired its outsize importance not because it was accurate, but because the media repeated it, exaggerated it, re-played it, made an indelible mantra of it. In the process, like a piece of trashy gossip that has made the rounds of the high school cafeteria—or like the myth that Anne Boleyn slept with her brother—it became stamped in viewers' minds as true.

The most famous of the stories told about Hillary was, of course, the email scandal. Even after Comey's exoneration, polling showed that 56 percent of Americans believed Clinton had indeed broken the law by relying on a personal email address. That number is ghastly, considering that she had in fact broken no laws, but they are unsurprising, given the overwhelming negative attention that network and cable news has paid to Clinton's emails—more airtime, as Mathew Yglesias reports, than to all policy issues combined. During the entire general election campaign, June 7 to November 8, Clinton only led over Trump in quantity of media coverage four times: once was when she had pneumonia, once was during the Democratic National Convention, and the other two were during and right after James Comey's announcements concerning her emails.

Thus, "a story that was at best of modest significance came to dominate the US presidential election,"[20] creating a misleading impression of Clinton's character and competence and vastly overshadowing coverage of both her accomplishments and her policy proposals. Is it any wonder that so many people had a totally false impression of what a Clinton presidency would be like? Between Sanders's labeling of Clinton as a Wall Street lackey and the GOP obsession with her emails—both of which were lavishly covered by the mass media—the Clinton campaign was defined by negative sound bites.[21]

I TRY (UNSUCCESSFULLY) TO TELL THE STORY

I was really nervous. I'd been on television before, but never about such a controversial issue, and for such a potentially broad audience. I imagined the interview would be the start of many others. It was April 2017, and the 2016 election was being discussed endlessly—that is, numerous panels were dissecting all the mistakes Hillary Clinton and/or her campaign and/or the Democratic National Committee had made. My book took a different approach and argued that a potent combination of factors, from GOP dirty tricks to Comey's eleventh-hour announcement was responsible. It was a perfect storm, and although Clinton's campaign wasn't without fault, so was the mainstream media, whose dislike and mistrust of Clinton colored their coverage, and so was Bernie Sanders, who branded Clinton as a tool of Wall Street.

It was a Saturday afternoon, and my interviewer was to be Sheinelle Jones. "Maybe Rachel Maddow will be next," said my friend and hairdresser, who also did my makeup for the occasion. Lots of eye makeup, and lots of foundation. "TV washes you out," she reminded me.

So there I was, early on Saturday afternoon, my hair freshly styled and my bottom perched on a high stool in a local

▶

TV station, fake landscape of Lexington, Kentucky in the background, earpiece plugged in to *MSNBC Live*. I had prepared for what I assumed were going to be some key questions about my argument in the book. But I guess my interviewer wasn't required to read the dust jacket of the book, let alone the book itself. And as for me, I clearly didn't get the memo that tells guests to always begin every response with "That's a good point." I almost fell off my stool when I heard the lead-in:

> Next up: The author of a new book argues that Clinton made one big mistake that probably cost her the presidency.

Was my earpiece plugged into Kellyanne Conway's universe of alternative facts?

No, there on the chyron, in bold letters: "CLINTON'S BIGGEST MISTAKE."

Since my book challenges the Clinton-blaming narratives so popular at the time, I was eager—while madly searching my own brain for a strategy to retort without being rude— to hear Sheinelle Jones's first question.

Ah. Clinton's "big mistake," Jones proposed, was that "she allowed the media to shape the narrative."

Allowed? With "EMAIL SCANDAL" and "CLINTON TRUST PROBLEM" headlined virtually every day, and with James Comey helpfully reminding us, just eleven days before the election, that the Trump's *Access Hollywood* tapes and the accusations of sexual abuse that followed were nothing compared to Clinton's email crimes—just what could she have done?

"You underestimate your own [that is, the media's] power," I said to Jones. (As I said, I didn't get the memo to begin with "That's a great point.") She didn't follow up on that, but quickly pivoted to her next prepared question, which was about the power of optics. Now, that is an actual argument of my book, and I was ready to talk about the readiness of the media, throughout the election, to headline "suspicious" appearances before the actual facts had become known. As in: "We don't know why Clinton needed to be helped into her car that day, but the optics aren't good. What is she hiding?"

Jones had in mind something different, though, and produced a video of a Trump rally, and those now-famous cries of "Lock her up, lock her up!" Pretty ugly, to be sure, but not what I meant when I wrote about optics. The Trump rally was a deliberately hate-rousing spectacle; it wasn't a "bad look" for him; that chant was exactly what he was going for. But I decided not to correct Jones's understanding and went with it, commenting on the blatantly misogynistic rhetoric of the clip. (I think, though, that I wasn't supposed to use the term "bitch" in quoting the epithets constantly thrown at Clinton because Jones looked uncomfortable. By now, she was likely regretting ever having agreed to have me on the show.)

She was determined, however, to get us back to a Clinton-blaming narrative, and produced a visual detailing the points made in a "blistering commentary" (as she put it) by Andrew Sullivan: Hillary Clinton put Trump in the White House, she mishandled her campaign, she spent too much time fund-raising, didn't visit the Rust Belt states, didn't communicate with the "working class." Blah blah blah.

I'd heard all of this many times, from the earliest postmortems on the results of the election. But what the hell, I'd give it one last try. So I said I didn't subscribe to Sullivan's narrative. I went on to remark that working-class people work, and have little time to follow hearings and speeches as they happen, but depend on the media's sound bites early in the morning and after work—and what they got from those fragments was far from the truth of Clinton's policies. I recalled, too, that Clinton had a remarkable 64 percent approval rating when she began her campaign, and by November had become—as she herself put it—"Typhoid Mary." Was that the result of not visiting Ohio during the last week of the election?

Then, of course, Jones and I were out of time. "We will be talking about this for a long time," she summed it all up.

▷

In fact, they didn't—talk about it, that is. Yes, once Russian interference became widely known, the anchors and pundits were willing to blame Russia, bots, fake internet pages—and occasionally, the print media (recently, the *New York Times* has come under fire.) But they fiercely (if unconsciously) still resist acknowledging, let alone analyzing, their own complicity—for example, in promoting the narratives that sunk Hillary. As I tried to get through to Sheinelle Jones, working people *work*—which means, for most, that they spend little time browsing Facebook, and get their news at breakfast and/or dinner, when the events of the day have been passed from show to show, anchor to anchor, much like a game of telephone, and by 6 o'clock have been "edited" in the process: certain items headlined and repeated, others shoved off the map. Inevitably some events (gaffes are favorites) get empowered and others (e.g. important exchanges in congressional hearings that don't fit into current narratives) never make it into popular consciousness. In this computer age, television still decides, for most people, what's newsworthy.

5 IF GEORGE ORWELL COULD CRITIQUE BROADCAST NEWS

I teach writing to graduate students. For about half the semester, I have to train them to unlearn every habit they've acquired in other classes. Jargon. Pretentious phrasing meant to show they "do theory." Insider codes. Abstract flights of unmoored words traipsing around in the academic heavens, winking and kissing each other, making everyone on the ground feel stupid.

For the past twenty years, Ralph Keyes's *The Courage to Write*[1] has been one of my indispensable guides. Keyes helps readers understand that much of what they thought was sophisticated scholarly prose actually generates "verbal fog"—the use of jargon and other forms of higher obfuscation—to obscure rather than clarify thought.

I have my students bring in a previously written piece, cross out all the foggy items, and try to replace them with ordinary English. Most are shocked to discover that once they declutter their writing, they often have no idea what they meant to say. It's a depressing but necessary exercise for which they are ultimately grateful. Once they've cleared away the fog, they can ask themselves what they are truly interested in writing about—and, in many cases, they rediscover why they wanted to write in the first place. That motivation often gets lost in the process of so-called professional training.

Another great guide is George Orwell's essay "Politics and the English Language,"[2] written in 1948 but more applicable today than ever. In fact, I find it so piercingly true that even though I've taught the piece for decades, I still fall in love with it every time.

The first rule of good writing, Orwell notes, is to remember that language as an instrument is "for expressing and not for concealing or preventing thought." Well, of course, you might be thinking. What else could language be for? In practice, however (and particularly in academia), we often use language as a kind of protective armor that makes us look smart and avoids any straight talk that would expose our confusion or not-yet-formed ideas. Expressing ideas precisely is hard. It's so much easier to grab a familiar phrase and insert rather than struggle to find just the right words. The trouble with these familiar phrases, though, is that all the life has been beaten out of them. What's left is empty verbal skin and none of the meat of meaning.

What we should be doing instead, according to Orwell, is "let the meaning choose the word, and not the other way around." He goes on, with a phrase that gives me chills every time: "In prose, the worst thing you can do with words is surrender to them."

I'm pretty sure that unless you've read "Politics and the English Language," this is the first time you've encountered the idea of surrendering to words. That's part of why it's so great. It catches us by surprise, unexpectedly putting together the emotionally charged idea of surrender with that quotidian little noun "word." But Orwell gives us more. Surrendering to words means "throwing your mind open and letting the ready-made phrases come crowding in. They will construct your sentences for you—even think your thoughts for you, to a certain extent—and at need they will perform the important service of partially concealing your meaning even from yourself."

The verbal fog of academese is a species of surrender to words, but not the only one. Political writing, Orwell argues (in fact, it's his main target), suffers from a similarly stale, imprecise, essentially clubby embrace of prefabricated phrases, repetitious metaphors that have been bludgeoned to death, pretentious verbal tics, and other enemies of clarity and communication. "As soon as certain topics are raised," Orwell writes, "no one seems able to think of turns of speech that are not hackneyed: prose consists less and less of words chosen for the sake of their meaning, and more and more of phrases tacked together like the sections of a prefabricated hen-house."

Orwell wasn't thinking of broadcast punditry when he wrote these words, of course, but of political pamphlets, articles, manifestos, and speeches. Television was in an experimental stage in 1948, and for many years after played a tiny thirty-minute role as a conveyer of news. Today the talking heads never shut up—even when there is little actual news to report or when they have already reported it ten times—and prefabricated construction is the norm. After I heard MSNBC's Kristen Welker use the word "robust" four times in a two-minute report, I decided to turn my annoyance into a game. I asked my Facebook and Twitter friends which words and phrases they would most like to see purged from the media's vocabulary. I wasn't surprised that each was an example of one of Orwell's top enemies of thought.

Dying Metaphors

"Worn out metaphors which have lost all evocative power and are merely used because they save people the trouble of inventing phrases for themselves."

- Baggage
- Getting out over one's skis (very popular at the moment)
- Speaking truth to power (especially when said about someone who is in a position of power)
- Rockstar (when applied to a politician)
- Teachable moment

- Horse race (when applied to contest for political office)

- At the end of the day

- Unpack

- Our better angels

- Thrown under the bus

Some of these all-too-familiar turns were once vibrant. "Unpack," for example, used to be exclusive to the vocabulary of analytic philosophers. among whom it meant excavating and laying out clearly the individual components of something (as in "Let's unpack that argument"). When journalists picked it up, it evoked a visual image that had some life, suggesting that ideas were like suitcases, stuffed full of various items to be sorted rather than singular in nature.

"Our better angels" was evocative and lovely when President Barack Obama quoted Abraham Lincoln, and (unlike the Gettysburg Address) Lincoln's inaugural address was new to many people. ("We are not enemies, but friends. We must not be enemies. Though passion may have strained, it must not break our bonds of affection. The mystic chords of memory will swell when again touched, as surely they will be, by the better angels of our nature.") And "speaking truth to power" was both passionate and precise as the title of Anita Hill's memoir. Today, however, all these phrases are as common as punctuation marks.

More disturbing than the simply overused phrases are those that influence how listeners organize their perceptions. When a politician is anointed a "rock star," for example, it immediately casts a certain sheen over him (I've yet to hear "rock star" applied to a woman) and immediately makes viewers want to come to the party. Political rock stars are as much, if not more, the creation of the media as any groundswell, yet pundits continually describe such stardom as though they are reporting a natural phenomenon.

Another example: describing a political contest as a "horse race" confers a kind of equality to the contestants, even if one is a thoroughbred and the other a show pony. It also creates a sense of breathless anticipation. Who is gaining? Who is falling behind? Are they neck and neck? All of this makes position in the polls seem far more important than, say, policy differences.

Verbal False Limbs

Basically, padding that adds nothing to a sentence except excess syllables.

- Quite frankly (rarely used to indicate that a particularly frank or candid statement is coming; reporters have become addicted to peppering their sentences with this)
- The fact of the matter

- With all due respect

- It remains to be seen

- Look or So (as the first word of the answer to a question, serving no purpose other than to create the illusion of dialogue)

Pretentious Diction

The examples Orwell gives are drawn from science, history, Greek, Latin, and foreign phrases. His essay preceded the importing of academic jargon into mainstream journalism. When I was in college, newscasters talked like regular people, and it was a relief to come home from my class on post-structuralism, turn on the television, and not have to ponder what "hegemony" really meant. No more. In fact, some of MSNBC's regulars—Chris Hayes comes immediately to mind—occasionally forget that they are not in a college lecture hall, discoursing about theory.

As an academic trained in philosophy and critical theory, I recognize these words and their origins: "Deconstruct" comes from a school of French philosophy. Journalists often use it as synonymous with "unpack," which it is not—to "deconstruct" is not simply to break down into parts but to show that what is thought to be universal or timeless is in fact historically "constructed." "Narrative" comes from literary criticism, and has actually been pretty useful to broadcasters, now that most news is presented encased in an evolving story. "Epistemological" comes from classical philosophy, and is almost always misused by broadcasters, who throw it around indiscriminately anytime they want to sex up any discussion involving issues concerning facts, lies, truth, and so on. In philosophy, it refers to the *domain* of knowledge: what can and can't be known, what knowledge is. Broadcast news doesn't fly that meta, not even on Chris Hayes's show (although the word "meta" itself gets tossed around).

Especially during the past five years or so, academic language has become a goldmine for broadcast news. "Existential" is frequently used, incorrectly, to mean "threatening continued life" rather than, as for French philosophers, the inescapable conditions of existence. I thought I had escaped "performative" when I retired from teaching, where it appears at least once a page in every student paper (not their fault, it's in all their instructors' articles, too). But no—I even heard Chuck Todd use it. And most irritating, there is the ever-mutilated "Other" (see also "Othering," "Othered," "The Other"). I'm fairly sure most of my undergraduates, for whom the term has become a political grenade to throw at the "unwoke," have no idea that the concept was the brainchild of Simone de Beauvoir, and that "woman" was the paradigmatic, historically ubiquitous "Other."[3] Her discussion is elegant and subtle and it's not surprising it has been taken up by many disciplines and used to apply to any group that is described or treated as belonging to a secondary—or possibly even non-human—form of life. But she would have cringed at the word "othering" as well as its use as an accusation to establish the progressive credentials of the accuser. ("Othering" has gotten so out of hand that I had a student accuse me of "othering" her because I misspelled her name, which she took as deliberately erasing her ethnicity.) Any time Michael Eric Dyson is on as a guest, you can be sure some variant of "Other" will come up.

Not all broadcaster jargon is theoretical or political in origin but seems to carry the simpler thrill of being more literary than straight talk. "Resonates," "problematic" "contested," "granular," "inflection point." Broadcasters also love describing ideas, movements, arguments, and the like with words that in everyday discourse usually belong to the world of physical bodies: "nimble," "appetite," and "robust" are three of those.

Meaningless Words

Orwell is referring to words that are so plastic and have such variable meanings that they wind up with no accepted meaning at all and are thus used—sometimes deceptively—any way the speaker wants.

The most glaring contemporary example I can think of is "establishment," which "the Left" (another phrase that fits the bill) still throws around with passion. But it's not just the Left that is guilty. Bernie Sanders may have originally tossed the grenade, but commentators and anchors from left, right, and center have passed it from hand to hand casually and recklessly, seemingly unaware that although the word is a dud meaningwise, it can cause extensive damage as a weapon of political destruction.

Its so-called opposite, "progressive," is among Orwell's own examples, and pundits now use it (in a contrast with "centrist" or "moderate") to designate different wings of Democrats. They then distribute politicians with basically similar agendas and ideals under one column or another, creating the illusion of major differences. In 2015 and 2016, they smushed together Trump and Clinton with false equivalences; now they've turned Democrats into competing camps by labeling some "progressive" and some "centrist."

A couple of other provocative labels that have no commonly accepted meaning but are powerful shapers of how prospective voters imagine their choices: "insurgent" and "populist." Orwell calls this kind of self-serving shell game—in which honorific or demonizing labels appear wherever they are placed—a swindle.

During the Great Swindle of the 2016 election, broadcast news went all post-modern on us, and "narrative" and "optics" became standard pundit vocabulary. Why were journalists suddenly talking like English professors? I guess it felt fresh and somehow sexy to stop reporting what happened—the old-fashioned point of the news—and begin talking about what academics used to call the construction of reality. This is the study of how things are put together and shaped for various ends; the impact of how they appear and the impressions they create, rather than boring old facts.

But optics are not facts and reporting on optics with the same urgency and repetitive emphasis as facts is to create, for listeners or readers, a secondary world of faux realities as vivid and evidentiary as what actually took place.

No, I don't think the mainstream media is a generator of fake news. But by allowing the journalistic fashions of the moment to displace the rigor of distinctions, precision, and the difference between appearance and fact, mainstream media has softened the ground in which the Trumpian garden of lies could plant itself and flourish.

Trump convinced an awful lot of people that Mueller's investigation was a "witch hunt" simply by saying the words over and over, as journalists have called out. What they haven't acknowledged is that repetitively describing Russian interference as "meddling" has arguably shaped people's understanding by underplaying the seriousness of what happened. Meddling is what an interfering old relative does. The Russians very likely altered the course and outcome of a presidential election.

Euphemisms and Clichés

Orwell doesn't have a specific category for either of these, but they are clearly part of the surrender to words that is the main topic of his piece, and my Facebook and Twitter friends mentioned them frequently.

- Troubling (surely what's happening today is worth a little more concern than that)

- Give a listen (sit back in your rocking chair, suck on your corncob pipe, and hear POTUS mangle law, language, and morality)

- Hotly contested (please don't change the channel; this is exciting stuff)

- Highly anticipated (ibid)

- Hopes and prayers (it was painful, yet I was glad to see the parent of a recent school shooting victim tell the politicians, although not in exactly these words, to shove their hopes and prayers up a bodily orifice and get rid of guns)

- Misspoke (instead of "lied")

- Racially charged (instead of "racist")

- Unprecedented (we know that all bets are off, all rules have been broken, under Trump)

Post-Orwellian Fog: Zingers and Gaffes

Ever since Kennedy-Nixon, debates have held an absurd amount of power in electoral politics. What happened then is legendary: Kennedy had been well prepared with a set of talking points and was instructed to turn the questions around (nowadays, we call this a "pivot") in order to get his prepared points out no matter what the question was. Nixon, on the other hand, was a debate purist who addressed the questions with precision but had no winning sound bites; in addition he had a painful staph infection in his leg, and despite looking drawn and thin and sporting a five-o'clock shadow, refused makeup. Kennedy, who had been out campaigning in an open convertible in the California sun, didn't need any makeup, and Nixon, not wanting to be bested by Kennedy (and possibly, thinking of makeup as too feminine), said no. And then, too, there was Nixon's flop sweat and Kennedy's handsome features. The visual contrast was painful—and powerful. People who heard the debate on the radio thought that Nixon had won. But Don Hewitt knew better. "My God," he said when the debate ended, "we don't have to wait for election night. I just produced a television show that elected a president of the United States."[4]

Since then, what registers most from the debates are the zingers and gaffes, replayed endlessly by the pundits, and trivialities of appearance and manner: Lloyd Bentsen's squashing of Dan Quayle: "I served with Jack Kennedy. I knew Jack Kennedy. Jack Kennedy was a friend of mine. Senator, you're no Jack Kennedy"; Reagan's pivot on the issue of age; Dukakis's bloodless response to the question of whether or not he would favor the death penalty if his wife Kitty were raped and murdered (he held to his position, without any display of emotion or ambivalence); Obama's "You're likable enough, Hillary" (which arguably cost him the next day's primary election); Rick Perry's failure to remember the third government agency he wanted to eliminate ("Oops!"). And then, too, there are the commentators' declarations about who looked confident or nervous—Amy Klobuchar's quivering bangs branded as a sign of nervousness; Hillary Clinton's always thorough, careful answers described by Chuck Todd as "overprepared." The panel of questioners phrase questions designed to pit candidates against each other, and for weeks before a debate, commercials prepare viewers to be on the lookout for who will have their moment and who will get knocked out of the ring. Then, when the debates inevitably turn into gotchas, they take no responsibility for inclining the discourse in that direction. On nonsense like this, a presidency can turn.

It has little to do with who would best serve us as POTUS, and it can turn for or against a candidate on the whims of reporters. During the second Democratic debate this year, no doubt encouraged to have a "moment," Kamala Harris sharply rebuked Joe Biden for his earlier stand on busing. Invoking her own history as a little girl who stood waiting to be bused across town. Kamala's "I was that little girl" both disarmed and charmed. It was dramatic, it was unexpected. (What? This gorgeous, impeccably dressed woman was once a little Black girl?) And it caught Joe off guard. Kamala was rewarded with an initial surge in ratings and funding, and much talk about her "rising star." But Joe Biden was beloved by many older Democrats, particularly older Blacks, and Kamala was so . . . uh . . . *aggressive*. It didn't take long for the image of the Mean Prosecutor[5] viciously "attacking" Uncle Joe to supplant sympathy for the little girl, and for the narrative to get turned against Kamala. Soon the headlines were declaring her campaign unravelling and sinking (demonstrated by sliding poll numbers, mostly from the very white early primary states), and we were told that in addition to various strategic campaign mistakes, she didn't connect with Black voters. Yes, I even heard Reverend Al Sharpton say that on TV!

I wonder, though, just how many Black voters actually got to know Kamala. Those videos that showed her playful side—which often embodied vibrant aspects of her Blackness—were mostly buried in Facebook, Instagram, and Twitter pages, where she was often captured on video playing with kids, exuding the pleasure in life that made Joyful Warrior an appropriate nickname for her. She connected with plenty of Black (and white) women through those videos. I don't remember, though, seeing any of them on television. Her attack on Joe Biden, on the other hand, was headlined for working people as they drank their morning coffee, and even followed Kamala post-primary; as Biden deliberated on his choice of Vice-President, detractors of Harris criticized her "lack of remorse" for "excoriating" Joe Biden during the debate.[6]

The media took no responsibility for any of it: not for the panel's questioning, which pitted the participants of the debate against each other and encouraged the production of fatal blows and game-changing exchanges; not for the descriptions of Kamala as viciously attacking Biden (surely a gendered double standard being applied here, which I don't recall being applied to Bernie when he blasted Clinton for numerous corporate crimes against working people); and not for the metaphors that painted Kamala as having had her moment until her campaign unraveled.

My Kamala example has a gendered—and perhaps a racial—dimension, but the problem is more general. It won't be easy, but we need to find some way of tempering the media's freedom with a sense of responsibility for the realities that are created in the process of exercising that freedom. To start, media needs to get rid of the illusion that they are merely reporting the news. Choices are constantly being made and while some of them are invaluable, others—like giving expansive airtime to every Trump rally, every tweet, every lie—are destructive. It's more than a little late, but if we come through his presidency having learned that discriminative judgment is not equivalent to censorship, that not everything can be balanced with another side, and that not everything is fit to air—that will be a good thing.

6 INTERSECTIONS OF TV, "REALITY," AND REALITY

The Transformation of Donald Trump

Donald Trump's time as President is often casually referred to as a reality show. Commentators never explain exactly what they mean by this. Perhaps they have in mind that Trump's presidency is performance rather than real. We all know by now that much of reality television is set up, staged, and heavily edited, and when Trump told us that he could be more presidential than anyone, he clearly signaled that he imagined it as a role to take on, perhaps not so different than the wise, managerial mogul he played in *The Apprentice*. Or perhaps commentators have in mind, paradoxically, the surreality of our lives under Trump: we still can't believe that we actually elected this man—and continue, despite the corruption, the lies, the outrageous incompetence, the blatant racism, to engage in normal life, most of the time. There I am, in the grocery store, trying to find the gluten-free lasagna noodles—and Donald Trump is in the White House! Or maybe, in calling the Trump Show a reality show, pundits are simply acknowledging that the only way to make sense of any of it is to think of it as television rather than a presidency. Trump certainly does; he measures the success of his presidency by the ratings of his TV appearances.

Maybe political commentators consider it too low-life a form of entertainment to waste their time on, but I've yet to hear one actually talk about *The Apprentice*—the reality show that made Trump's rise possible—or consider how the genre (or more precisely, genres) of the reality show itself evolved over the years to pave the way for Trump, to inure us to the level of meanness, self-interest, bragging, and unapologetic narcissism that he exhibits every day. I, however, have followed reality shows from the first *Real World* through most of the *Housewives*, and for a time was a regular viewer of *Celebrity Apprentice*. I could say it was required for my job teaching popular culture and media—and that's true—but it's only partly true. I don't have to explain the other reasons I watch, do I? They are probably pretty much the same reasons other television junkies watch.

My bad habits, however, have equipped me to comment with more precision—and increasing annoyance—about the role of reality television as theorized by many cultural scholars. The fact is that for the most part, cultural theorists and television critics just don't watch enough television to comment about it with authority. So James Poniewozik inaccurately describes Donald Trump as the villain of *Celebrity Apprentice*: "blunt, impolite," "bellicose," and an "apex predator who knew how to get things done."[1] Like many other commentators, Poniewozik finds those qualities crystallized in the culminating "You're fired," which came at the climax of every show. For Poniewozik, there's not much of a step from the Trump of Apprentice to the Trump of the presidential rallies.

Anyone who watched the show regularly, however, knows that Trump fired most contestants reluctantly, often prefacing the famous phrase with compliments and regrets. He left it to the contestants to provide the squabbling cutthroat relations that viewers had come to expect from those fighting tooth and nail to remain on the island. Trump himself was calm, generous with praise, gentle with criticism, and above all impersonal in his decisions. No animus, just matter-of-fact appreciation of, for example, the importance of branding, or the necessity of holding the project manager responsible. Often "he would pause uncomfortably and soften his voice just before he sacked a contestant,"[2] constructing a "new public persona" that "artfully blended his love of power with a glimmer of humility [and] a touch of self-deprecating humor."[3] Flanked by Ivanka and Don Jr., far cooler (read: virtually robotic) in their roles as advisers to their dad, they played the unemotional dispenser of business savvy. Trump, on the other hand, was not the snarling boss but the sympathetic but firm father who hated to punish the contenders, but really had no choice.

The racist, bullying Trump of his rallies did not evolve from his reality television persona, as Poniewozik argues. Except for the ever-present brandishing of himself as the pinnacle of success, the Trump of the rallies was yet another new character for Donald to play—and one, I suspect, that allowed his anger and narcissism to become extravagantly and dangerously unleashed as his previous personae had not. And surprise! It turned out that many others were ripe for encouragement to indulge every Id-driven impulse, every "fuck you" to the politically correct, every revenge on the women who had humiliated them.

I suspect Trump himself was genuinely surprised at how voraciously his supporters gobbled up the permission he gave them to let loose with the purest, most vicious rancor. When that Trump then gave the OK for every vile impulse to assert itself against elite restraint the combination was irresistible: *Father Knows Best* meets "I'm mad as hell and I'm not gonna take it anymore." Recall that the line that drew the most whoops of delight during the first Republican debate was Trump's takedown of "political correctness" as the ruin of the culture—not immigrants themselves, but the prohibition against being anti-immigrant. It's an important distinction, I think, because the latter touches deeper recesses of resentment, the frustrations and angers that go back to being a child not allowed to do and say bad things. You don't have to be good little boys and girls, someone was finally preaching; say what you feel, do what you feel like, don't let the goody-two-shoes liberals (read: mama Hillary) boss you around.

In this way, Trump's relationship with his supporters got at their most infantile desires, and was perfectly in keeping with the release of the Id and a fuck you to the parental Ego that was happening in other areas of the culture.

The *Real World* and *Real Housewives*

You can see it most dramatically by comparing the 1992 season of *The Real World*, arguably the first contemporary style "reality show," with the last season, appropriately titled "Bad Blood." I show episodes from the two seasons in my class, and the students are astounded at how slow, unsexy, and boring the first season appears to them. Although the show begins with the tease that viewers will be watching what happens when seven strangers stop being polite and get real, in fact the members of the household are all really nice, supportive kids who by the standards of 2013 are always polite with each other. There are crushes and flirtations, but no sexual hookups. No one engages in even the mildest form of physical violence. And perhaps most striking, they deal with the racial and gender differences among them in a tolerant, "let's talk about it" way. When Southern girl Julie commits what today would be seen as a race crime, worthy of eviction—rapper Heather's beeper goes off, and Julie asks if she sells drugs—Heather is less insulted than struck by Julie's naivety and takes it upon herself to instruct Julie on what various words and phrases mean in rap lyrics. "She doesn't understand" is her attitude, and the two become friends. There are long sessions devoted simply to talk around the table, exploring their experiences and ideas. It's like *My Dinner with Andre* for young adults.

And predictably, it got my students yawning and impatient. "Bad Blood" woke them up, though. From the first episode, people are getting naked, bragging about their sexual appeal, evaluating the asses of others, and a security guard is required to break up a threateningly violent fight (about something trivial that I can no longer even remember—and I saw it again yesterday). But the producers, not content to let the sex and fights develop organically, insert a twist to insure that bad blood rather than friendship will be the ruling principle: just as the original seven are settling in (picking out fuck partners, routinely insulting each other in the confessional room, the men working on their absurdly muscled bodies) seven people from the past with whom the original seven have unresolved issues are brought in. There are exes, there are relations, there are past betrayals, lies—the list goes on.

Early episodes of *The Real World*, only lightly edited, presented characters sympathetically and had the feel of documentaries. When audiences smelled a setup or felt a character was being racially stereotyped, it provoked moral outrage. But by 2013, hair-pulling fights, rampant alcoholism, and sleazy story lines are incited and developed. Contestants get into physical fights that are allowed to go on without interference. (Who would interfere with such good TV?) And the sexual hookups commence with the first episode.

Similarly, in *The Real Housewives* series, the bitch is loose. Post-war popular culture had its share of scheming vixens on *Dallas*, *Dynasty*, and the rest. But they played a supporting role to Mary Tyler Moore, Claire Huxtable, Murphy Brown, the Designing Women, and other independent but likeable prime-time women—and they clearly were marked as villainesses. Nowadays, really, really mean girls, back-stabbing frenemies, and defiantly materialistic sluts are not just dots on the landscape, but truly in the ascendancy. And unlike Alexis Carrington, they don't even scheme in secret. They're proud of their materialism and their aggression, which Bravo highlights in the self-defining snippets that

FIGURE 7 *The Real World*, Episode One: More a talkfest than a slugfest. MTV.

FIGURE 8 *The Real World: Bad Blood*: Sex, fights, and bodies, bodies, bodies. MTV.

open each of their Housewife shows ("If it doesn't make me money, I'm not interested in it" . . . "There may be younger housewives, but no-one is hotter than me" . . . "I don't try to keep up with the Joneses; I am the Joneses"). Women crave power, hell yes! And they lust over designer shoes and handbags. And yes, they will beat each other up, verbally and physically—call each other whores, pull each other's wigs off, overturn tables—given half the chance.[4]

Whether they are competing with their nails out on *The Bachelor* or hurling insults at each other (and sometimes threatening physical violence) on the "reunion" shows of *The Real Housewives*, the women of reality television, apparently, have no impulse control whatsoever, which makes them highly prized by an unhinged consumer culture that gratifies all purchasable tastes, no matter how sleazy or degrading.

Perhaps from the very beginning, but certainly since Trump released the unvarnished, voracious Id—male style—into presidential politics, the behavior of the housewives may not seem all that awful to many viewers. Ideas move fast from conception to materialization in consumer culture, and as they find their audience, they gather steam. A door is opened, taboos are lifted, something sounds a resonant note with buyers, and within short order much more is permitted—even celebrated—than would have been dreamed of five years before. Susan Herbst, in *Rude Democracy*, says, in speaking about the escalation of vicious attacks among politicians and from news commentators, that "conflict sells and excites in a way that calm political dialogue never will."[5] Our polarized political discourse, by the time the *Housewives* aired in 2006, had already degenerated into name-calling. And the internet had teased the bitch out in the rest of us, enabling "users to lash out at individuals without forethought." Laura Stepp, at the *Huffington Post*, makes an apt comparison: "Tweets, blog posts and comments on Facebook are like the wicked notes girls used to pass in high school but are read by a much larger audience."[6] It's no accident that the housewives all have their own blogs, in which they stoke each other's fires between episodes. These sorts of blogs, David Denby points out in *Snark*, encourage nastiness to "metastasize as a pop writing form: a snarky insult, embedded in a story or post, quickly gets traffic; it gets linked to other blogs; and soon it has spread like a sneezy cold through the vast kindergarten of the Web."[7]

The metastasis went much further, though, than Denby could have predicted, when in 2016 a snotty, entitled con-man spat snark and sleaze all over the presidential debates, and ultimately flipped the White House as unceremoniously as Theresa flipped over the table in a New Jersey restaurant.

The Best Feminist Moment from Seventies TV

Advertising is essentially amoral. It's less interested in being ethical or politically correct than it is in developing as wide and diverse a consumer group as possible. In the fifties, the targeted audience was assumed to be white, middle class, and Christian, and the advertiser was a draconian dictator of content, not just of ads but of the shows themselves. Westinghouse, the sponsors of *The Adventures of Ozzie and Harriet*, insisted on lots of kitchen scenes to show off the sparkling appliances made possible by post-war productive capabilities. (How Ozzie—or Jim Anderson or any of the suburban dads—could afford the appliances featured on the shows is a mystery, as they were always home, often sitting around the kitchen table reading the paper. "It was always Saturday" in those houses, said Hugh Beaumont, who played the hubby on Donna Reed.) Today, many of the prohibitions seem absurd: When Camel sponsored the NBC news show, "You could not use a NO SMOKING sign. You could not show a picture of a camel. You could not show anybody smoking a cigar" and of course you couldn't mention cancer. "If a person died of cancer," Arthur Holch recalls, it was "of a long illness." The broadcast ended with a large triangular ashtray, with a cigarette burning in it, and a Camel carton in the background. Camel also refused to have cigar-smoking celebrities like Groucho Marx on the nightly news—the one exception being Winston Churchill.[8]

Of course, television doesn't just advertise, but is *itself* an advertisement. The traditional American family the early sitcoms were aimed at was, of course, a fantasy. Those kitchens were aspirational: designed to encourage consumers to want to become as much like the Cleavers as possible. In the gap between the televised image and the reality of the American family was the potential for profits. Who cared whether Black families didn't see their lives reflected? The assumption was that they couldn't afford to have a house like the Cleavers, with their gleaming appliances. Working women? The post-war period, as has been well documented, was intent on getting them into those kitchens—or carrying a Budweiser into the backyard, where Dad was snoozing on a hammock.

But there is another side to the amorality of television than the advertising of mythical ideals. The paradox of the amoral profit motive is that while it can create habits that make people ill and can certainly reinforce (what are perceived as) traditional values, it needs to remain alert to emerging trends and previously ignored demographics. And those discoveries can promote progressive changes. Whenever my students complain about capitalism, I remind them that the beautiful Black models that now fill the pages of *Vogue* are not the products of progressive-minded executives, but of the recognition that bypassing the needs of Black women was to ignore a potentially huge market. We're seeing this happen now with plus-size models, too. (Plus-size is actually more the norm for American women than model-thin. Incredible that it took so long to recognize this!) The recognition of class diversity within other diversities (e.g. there were actually well-heeled gay men with lots of money to spend, duh) opened the door to more erotic representations of the male body in mainstream publications. And these eventually transformed what straight men wanted to look like, too.

When the first mixed race family appeared in a 2013 Cheerios commercial (the little girl spills Cheerios over her snoozing daddy's chest to "help his heart") the fact that the daddy of the adorable little girl is revealed to be Black was met with applause by some but outrage by others. Some viewers wrote on Facebook that they found the commercial disgusting and that it made them want to vomit. Today, it's hard to spot a commercial—from cereal to cars—that doesn't feature multiracial and, increasingly, gay families. In fact, it's hard to spot an all-white family anymore in a TV ad. The deliberateness of it is laughable. (bell hooks once joked that if the numbers of black female judges in real life actually equaled the number on TV, we'd be set.) The ads, like the election of our first Black president, may create the illusion that we've come much farther than we have. Nonetheless, the fact is that when my daughter watches television, she sees many families that look like hers (except for the advanced age of her parents). And thanks to Shondra Rhimes, creator of *Grey's Anatomy* and *How to Get Away with Murder*, she's learned that she doesn't have to be Tyra Banks or Beyoncé Knowles into order to have a love life. Television can be tyrannical in advertising mythical lifestyles; but it can also act as an affirming mirror for the previously ignored or denigrated—and, in the bargain, create a more inclusive world of representations.

Most of the time, then, the politics of television is a mixed bag, as it tries to attract emerging or previously ignored viewers while at the same time remaining appealing to more traditional ones. Discussing the history of representations of women and feminism, Susan Douglas describes this as the media "tak[ing] away with one hand what they had just given us with the other." So in the early seventies we were given the thrilling catharsis of Bea Arthur's *Maude*, a woman who spoke her mind and refused to obey gender conventions— but who in the process dominates and bullies her husband, reinforcing the stereotype of the feminist as a strident, loud, unfeminine bruiser. At the other end of the continuum was *The Mary Tyler Moore Show*, which broke ground for the single working woman who lived alone (luckily for Mary Richards, with great neighbors) and even took birth control pills (!), but tempered her independence with stammers, blushes, and deference to Mr. Grant, her boss.

In 1988, when *Murphy Brown* premiered, we were in the midst of the Reagan era—not exactly a feminist utopia, but it did put a lot of women in business suits with linebacker shoulder pads, brand new briefcases, and a lack of guidance as to how to behave in these professional, high-voltage worlds previously barred to us. In that context, Murphy was an inspiration: the opposite of a pushed-around, silenced woman, she wore those sharply tailored suits and the power that came with them as if born to do so. Unlike her fore-sister Mary Richards, she obeyed no one's marching orders. (True, a 25-year-old guy nominally ran the newsroom; it was always clear, however, who was emotionally and intellectually the boss.) Murphy didn't have to force it, either—it emanated naturally from her character.

Murphy (Candice Bergen) didn't even notice any glass ceilings—she'd already shattered the internal ones that Mary Richards, for all her spunk, kept ramming against. When during the 1991 season she got pregnant and had a baby—without a husband—Dan Quayle was morally outraged at the challenge to family values (especially the message it sent to poor, inner city women). Yet Murphy defiantly gave "all the traditional stereotypes about motherhood the raspberries. And continued, even after the birth of her child, to be as insensitive, narcissistic, and bossy as before."[9]

But although Murphy was gender transgressive in personality and hierarchy (*People* called her a "merciless careerist")[10] the show rarely commented on feminist issues. Rather, as Bonnie Dow describes her, Murphy is "postfeminist" insofar as she is presented as the *product* of feminism—a successful career woman who doesn't feel the need to act feminine—rather than a critic of patriarchy. In contrast, while the women of *Designing Women* were in no way masculine in dress or personality, at least two of them made explicit feminist arguments about the resilience of sexism and male dominance; in this way it's by some accounts a far more feminist show.

Nowhere is this clearer than in the two shows' respective responses to the Clarence Thomas–Anita Hill hearings. While Murphy went metaphorical, in an episode where she is called to appear before a Senate committee (on media leaking— no mention at all of harassment or indeed of any gender issue) and criticizes the "grandstanding and shameless self-promotion" of the male senators at the (fictional) hearing, *Designing Women* presents a feminist commentary on the actual hearing, including clips of Thomas and Hill. Mary Jo (Annie Potts) wears a T-shirt emblazoned with "HE DID IT" and Julia Sugarbaker (Dixie Carter) stormily takes on the arguments and comments made against Hill. Although the show represents the other point of view (Carlene wears a T-shirt insisting "SHE LIED"), it's done via the show's ditzes Alison (Julia Duffy) and Carlene (Jan Hooks), who are made fun of, and lest one is still confused about the show's politics, it ends (well, almost ends) after Thomas is confirmed, with a rousing speech by Mary Jo in which she—gasp—even uses the term "feminist":

All we want is to be treated with equality and respect. Is that asking too much? I'm sorry, I don't mean to be strident and overbearing, but, you know, nice just doesn't cut it anymore. I'm mad because we're fifty-one percent of the population and only two percent of the United States Senate . . . I'm mad because in a Seminole, Oklahoma, police station, there's a poster of a naked women that says "women make bad cops." I'm mad because in spite of the fact that we scrub America's floors, wash the dishes, have all the babies, and commit very little of the crime, still we only make fifty-eights cents on the dollar. I don't know about the rest of you women out there, but I don't give a damn anymore if people think that I'm a feminist or a fruitcake.[11]

Designing Women, long before Christina Yang and Meredith Grey were each other's "person," was a show situated almost entirely within a family-like world where the bonds between women were foremost (and unlike *Grey's Anatomy*, there weren't even any McDreamys or McSteamys to compete with those bonds). In the episode "The Strange Case of Anita Hill and Clarence Thomas," writer Susan Bloodworth-Thomason brought a nonfictional woman into that world and let us know unequivocally where the show stood. Sure, "feminist or fruitcake" came with a laugh track, but the episode ended with a pastiche of clips from the hearing and a final still photograph. The clips: Arlen Spector accusing Hill of lying; John Danforth calling her an "erotomaniac"; John Doggett portraying her as a woman bitter over unrequited love for

FIGURE 9 *Designing Women*: Not afraid to be feminist. Shown: Annie Potts. CBS.

Thomas; the swearing in ceremony, with Bush's declaration that America is founded on the idea that all men are created equal. The concluding still: a shot of Anita Hill herself, silent. I can't remember whether I clapped or sat with jaw clenched; I do remember that it was the first time I felt a sitcom had passed through the wall of "it's just a TV show" and reached out to me.

Watching the episode again in 2020, I was amazed not only at what an explicit feminist point of view it took, but how instructive it dared to be. This was a sitcom, after all (part of a Monday "women's night" lineup designed as an alternative to *Monday Night Football*), and yet much of the script referred, with specificity, to what was actually said and done at the hearing. Much of that was so outrageous that it *was* funny—but the viewer was never let off the hook and allowed to simply laugh, because it all *did* happen. I could imagine Linda Bloodworth-Thomason (besides being the show's producer and writer, a friend and supporter of Hillary Clinton) saying to herself, "The hell with it. It'll be funny, but it's damn well going to make a serious point too. And it's going to be accurate, if only for the historical record."

What Brett Kavanaugh Learned from Clarence Thomas

Putting O. J's glove aside, The Hill-Thomas hearing was arguably the first time that an accused man—not to mention a candidate for the Supreme Court—so shamelessly exploited the fact that he was being televised. To begin with, Thomas arranged it so that his appearances were on a Friday night and Saturday, when audiences would be much larger, and—surprising Anita Hill, who had expected to appear after Thomas—made sure he got the last word. In his response, impassioned and furious, brimming with self-justification, Thomas claimed the charges—"This sleaze, this dirt"—were a politically motivated concoction, deliberately leaked to the media. "And this committee and this body," he went on, "validated it and displayed it in prime time over our entire nation."

> *This is a circus. It's a national disgrace. And from my standpoint, as a black American, it is a high-tech lynching for uppity blacks who in any way deign to think for themselves, to do for themselves, to have different ideas, and it is a message that unless you kowtow to an old order, this is what will happen to you. You will be lynched, destroyed, caricatured by a committee of the U.S. Senate rather than hung from a tree.*[12]

It was a brilliant strategy; the implication was that to vote against Thomas was to be a racist. But Thomas undoubtedly knew that besides the senators, thousands of male viewers were also watching, identifying and sympathizing with him, especially if they were Black. (The fact that Hill was also Black made no difference; in this scenario, she was "woman.") But women were watching, too, and many had the same reaction as Julia and Mary Jo to the humiliation of Anita Hill and privileging of Thomas's version of events. When I was sexually harassed by a professor in the 1970s, we didn't even have a word for it. But the scoffing dismissal of the male students, their pointing out that I "didn't exactly dress like a nun," and the chairman's permission for me to drop the course provided my reason was "personality differences," all came back when I watched the hearings. And I wasn't alone. Sexual harassment became a high-voltage topic of discussion, 1992 was declared the Year of the Woman (yes, we've had more than one of those) and a significant number of women (which some called "the Anita Hill Class") were elected to Congress.

We thought everything would change. But when in 2019 Supreme Court nominee Brett Kavanaugh defended himself against Christine Blasey Ford's charge that he had sexually assaulted her at a friend's house during high school, it was PTSD-time for second-wave feminists. Blasey Ford, if possible even more reserved than Anita Hill, had come forward reluctantly, and told her account without theatrics. She clearly wasn't comfortable with the eye of the nation on her, but she was so credible that after her appearance journalists were pronouncing Kavanaugh's confirmation doomed.

Kavanaugh, however, had learned a few tricks from Clarence Thomas. Claiming, unbelievably, that sex was a topic he never imagined would come up at a judicial confirmation hearing (apparently he was asleep while the rest of us were riveted—as the broadcasters liked to say— to our TVs during the Thomas-Hill hearings), he adopted Clarence Thomas's playbook as the outraged and aggrieved innocent. Actually, he went even further. While Thomas's words were full of fury, his performance style was contained. Kavanaugh shouted and sputtered and at various times dissolved into tears as he described the process as a national disgrace, a circus, and a deliberate attempt to destroy him. Though there was no metaphor as potent as "lynching,"

Kavanaugh's narrative drew on Trump's own favorite whine: the witch hunt:

> *You have tried hard. You've given it your all. No one can question your efforts. Your coordinated and well-funded efforts to destroy my good name and destroy my family will not drag me out. The vile threats of violence against my family will not drive me out. You may defeat me in the final vote, but you'll never get me to quit. Never.*[13]

I will spare the reader Kavanaugh's sentimental reminiscences about the calendar he kept during high school, his fondness for beer, the "goofy" things he did with his friends, the "disaster" that was his yearbook. And now, how his life was ruined: he "may never be able to coach again, never be able to teach again." Pass me my Kleenex.

My point? I have two, actually. The first is the impact that consciousness of the television camera has had on the way our congressional hearings are conducted. For those with entitled personalities, these cameras encourage extravagant acting out, with optics of far more importance than evidence: protesting their innocence, charging others with conspiracy, confident of being heard. For those of a more reticent personality, or who see their jobs as simple truth telling (like Robert Mueller—or Anita Hill, or Christina Blasey Ford) the inability or unwillingness to perform as though in a soap opera puts them at a distinct disadvantage. (But of course, a woman engaging in the theatrics of a Thomas or a Kavanaugh would be dismissed as an hysteric.)

FIGURE 10 What Brett Kavanaugh learned from Clarence Thomas. C-SPAN.

My second point is how extraordinary it is that almost thirty years after the Thomas-Hill hearings, we went through the same painful business again. Actually, the pretense of a fair trial was even worse with Kavanaugh. When politics are involved, I don't automatically assume sexual harassment or abuse charges are true. But I do expect them to be investigated thoroughly; letting the woman speak and then trashing her testimony without benefit of such an investigation is a farce, performed to create the illusion of respect for the woman's "perspective" without actually taking her charges seriously. This is just what happened with the Kavanaugh hearing, as an FBI investigation and the calling of witnesses was blocked by the Republican-controlled committee, reducing the proceedings to a "he said/she said" that they made sure Kavanaugh dominated. And this time, no prime-time network sitcom raised a fist against it.

7 TV DECONSTRUCTS GENDER

The Raw and the Cooked

So, our basement got flooded, and we were forced to move everything salvageable up to the sunroom, and then to sort out the items that were too mildewed from those to save. Among one of the boxes of my oldest books—I'm talking *Cherry Ames, Junior Nurse* here—I found some pages from a diary that I kept during 1962. I was fifteen. And among the pages gushing about how passionately in love I was with a boy named Joel, along with scornful comments about girlfriends who had decided to save themselves until marriage (I was a virgin myself but cultivating a cool girl persona), I found references to television shows I was looking forward to watching. I apparently really loved *Car 54, Where Are You?*—a comedy about two New York City cops that I now remember was extremely popular that year (it won an Emmy for prime-time comedy), but the most informative trip down my memory lane was an entry about men. Be forewarned and forgiving: my gender ontology here is NOT politically correct:

February 22, 1962:

All in all, I'm not happy but am in a sort of unthinking existentialistic [sic] state and am pretty content. Especially since tonight is "Dr. Kildare" which really is pretty damn lousy and I think he looks like a girl, but I get some kind of sadistic pleasure out of seeing things being operated on. Give me "Ben Casey" anytime! He's really a bitch, but he's real rough and resembles a man at least! My taste in men (in the entertainment field) is really weird. I go from Marlon to Yves Montand to George Chakiris to Warren Beatty in two minutes. I hate Victor Mature, Bert Parks, Rory Calhoun, The Everly Brothers, Pat Boone, Eddie Fisher, etc.

The "etc." contains the essence of what I was repelled by: referencing Claude Levi-Strauss, call it the cooked rather than the raw. (Marlon Brando: raw, especially in *Streetcar Named Desire*; Pat Boone: very, very cooked; Lassie: cooked; Rin-Tin-Tin: raw; Beatle John: raw; Beatle Paul: cooked.) My description of Joel (my real-life crush) bears out my preference for the raw: "He's fast and moody, and he mumbles instead of talking and everyone thinks he's ugly, but I think he is adorable." I liked bad boys, boys whose gristle hadn't yet been marinated by gentlemanly ideals. I liked boys who broke the rules. It's also true, unfortunately, that the raw boys were also the ones who treated me badly, and I know I'm not alone in that. There are many possible explanations, from lack of self-esteem to the belief, fostered by many movies, that if boys were mean to you it was because deep inside they really were attracted to you, to a confusion between the mean and the masculine. And then there's that enduring (and often toxic) fantasy that you would be the one to break through, to civilize the beast (without, of course, cooking out his or her sexual appeal). Because of course, there was vulnerability underneath the macho bravado, and you would release it—like Stella of *Streetcar*, who brought out the little boy in Stanley (Marlon Brando). I wrote about it in *The Male Body*, describing the famous scene in which Stella (Kim Hunter), sultry and erotically mesmerized, descends the stairs to their apartment:

> *At the bottom of the stairs is her husband Stanley, crying for her like a baby that's lost its mother, his muscular yet graceful back exposed, his T-shirt in shreds. A few moments before, he had beaten Stella in a rage . . . Now, realizing what he's done, he's distraught, beside himself with remorse. As Stella reaches the bottom of the stairs, he drops to his knees before her, and buries his head in her body. "Don't ever leave me, baby," he pleads; her hands run down the length of his back, then grasp his head, his hair, as she kisses him passionately.*[1]

Later, when Stella is in the hospital having her baby, Stanley rapes her sister Blanche, and the Production Code, headed by Roman Catholic Joseph Breen, enforcer of onscreen morality from 1934 until the mid-sixties, required that he be punished by having Stella, at the end, leave him—a change from the original that Williams reluctantly agreed to. In real life, however, it doesn't always happen that way. That's what *The Sopranos* exposed, and it's the source of its brilliance. No, Tony Soprano (James Gandolfini) doesn't rape anyone. He just murders people—and sometimes with his own hands, not by sending a Luca Brazzi out to do it for him—and he seems even to enjoy it. And although his wife leaves him for a time, at the end the family is together, eating at Holsten's. If he is to be narratively punished, it's not going to be Carmella who does it and for all we know— the last scene is ambiguous (Is he about to be whacked or not? The jury is out, and David Chase isn't telling)—he's going to get away with it all.

Tony Soprano and "College"

The fact that Tony Soprano, in 1999, inaugurated a new version of masculinity—one that boldly refuses to soften and make more palatable the violence that often goes along with the sexual (or any other) appeal of the raw—isn't apparent until the fifth episode of the first season, called "College." The writer David Chase knew it would be transgressive. *The Godfather* had Don Leone kill with his own hands only once, when he was a young immigrant (played by Robert De Niro) trying to establish himself in a neighborhood run by a greedy, less attractive Don. And once he is The Godfather (Marlon Brando) the film makes clear his biological family is his priority and justification for everything he does. When his son Michael loses touch with that, even going so far as to have his own brother killed, Coppola no longer bestows on him the affection that the first film brought to its depiction of Vito.

Tony Soprano, unlike Vito, likes the life, doesn't dream of legitimacy, and complains to his therapist Dr. Melfi (Loraine Bracco) that "the sun is setting over the empire," and that he's come in at the end rather than beginning. Until "College," we never see any real tenderness toward his children, and although he is troubled by panic attacks and mourns the leaving of a family of ducks from his pool, Tony is thoroughly coded as hyper macho, from the opening credit journey from the Lincoln Tunnel to his north Jersey McMansion ("the rings on Tony's meaty fingers, the thick dark hair on his forearms, the cigar between his teeth, the smoke trailing from his mouth as he checks the rearview mirror") to his casual but undeniable dominance over the other guys in his gang and his soldier, nephew Christopher (Michael Imperioli).

"College," however, whose frame is a trip with daughter Meadow (Jamie-Lynn Sigler) to check out colleges in Maine, reveals the side of Tony that is at the heart of the fantasy I described earlier, of the vulnerable sweetness that the right woman can release in the beast. In this case—

and I suspect it is this way for many men—that woman is his daughter. Throughout the episode, Tony affectionately hugs, playfully pokes, grabs her hand, and communicates pride to Meadow—smart enough to be admitted to the best colleges, but as beautiful as "those models on the cover of *Italian Vogue*"—as he tells her at a candlelit dinner at a New England restaurant. They are both dressed up, and the atmosphere and intimacy are more like a grown-up date than a meal between father and daughter. Twice during the episode they exchange heartfelt "I love you"s—not in itself unusual between parent and child—but both also remark on how special and unusual their relationship is. In fact, the relationship *is* unusual for Tony; he treats Meadow with an admiring respect that he doesn't lavish on any other women in his life (not even Dr. Melfi), so much so that when she asks if he is in the Mafia, he admits to her (as he hasn't to either Carmela or Dr. Melfi) that his work involves some "illegal gambling . . . and whatnot." They both know the admission is a delicate way of acknowledging that what she has suspected is true—an honesty that she rewards by contrasting him with the other boring, "full of shit" lawyer and executive dads of her friends, and praising that "you finally told the truth about this." (In the shooting script, she also says "And anyway, you're my sexy dad"—a line eliminated in the actual filming, no doubt because, given all the intimacy between them, it was too suggestive.)[2]

His behavior toward Meadow makes believable Carmela's (Edie Falco) confession to Father Phil Intintola that she still loves Tony and harbors the hope that he can change. We'd seen Tony the slob, in his underwear, eating prosciutto straight from the package at the family kitchen island. We'd seen him as the confident, surly boss of his men. We'd seen him brushing off his mistress. What we haven't seen is the sweetness that James Gandolfini brought to the role ("He's such a big guy, and yet he's such a sweetie pie," said Chase of his casting[3])—and that is undoubtedly part of what attracted Carmela to Tony when they first dated, and perhaps part of what keeps her with him, too. We see in "College" why women fall in love with him—not just for his raw masculinity, but for his courtliness. Win his respect (as Meadow has) and the beast becomes a prince.

But hold on. *The Sopranos* is not going to indulge the viewer in any fantasies of that kind. On the way to Bates College, at a gas station stop, Tony had spotted Febby Petrulio, who ten years earlier had been busted for selling heroin and flipped on Tony's father's friend Jimmy. Tony holds him responsible for his father's decline, and while Meadow is interviewing at Colby, chases Petrulio down and kills him—declining Christopher's offer to do it for him, and with a predatory violence that (as Matt Seitz and Alan Sepinwall put it) "makes it clear that this isn't some cute series about a henpecked Mob boss with troublemaking kids." Seitz and Sepinwall go on:

[B]ack in 1999, the effect of this particular killing was seismic. Four episodes in, viewers had seen murder and

violent death attributable to negligence or incompetence,
but Tony didn't commit any of these acts, nor was he
directly responsible for their occurrence . . . And although
it seemed unthinkable that hat he'd go through the
series without ordering at least one person's death—he's
toyed with the idea—a killing like this seemed equally
unthinkable, because TV protagonists didn't get down in
the muck like that. That was what henchman and guest
stars were for.[4]

Since the Sopranos, we've "watched countless protagonists
do horrible things," but this was the first. And while on a trip
with his daughter! (Chase initially imagined *The Sopranos*
primarily about the family, which would have appeal to
female viewers.)[5] As viewers, if afterward we still felt drawn
to Tony, then, like Carmela, we would be accepting a bargain
with the devil: the steep price of the magnetism (and promise
of protection) of raw masculinity. Sure, he could be tender
with his daughter, and genuinely adore her. But make no
mistake: Tony was a killer.

Screenwriter Matthew Weiner, watching the episode,
recognized how convention-shattering "College" was: "I just
turned to my wife," he recalls, "and said 'You do understand
what's going on here. This has never been done, that you
would take this hero and father of this TV show . . . and he's
going to strangle this guy with his bare hands. And we're
going to have to watch him next week and act like we care

FIGURES 11 AND 12 Two sides of Tony Soprano in "College." Shown: James Gandolfini and Jamie- Lynn Sigler. HBO.

about what's going on with him. That is revolutionary."[6] Revolutionary, yes—and also truer to life than the fantasy of reforming the beast, or the illusion that when the wife-batterer comes begging "Stella!" everything is gonna be alright from then on.

Don Draper and "Maidenform"

Weiner, in part inspired by *The Sopranos*, went on to create and write *Mad Men*, a show that deconstructs masculinity in a different but no less revolutionary way. Don Draper (Jon Hamm) isn't exactly raw, but he isn't exactly cooked either. Unlike Stanley or Tony, he'd never be caught dead eating deli meat with his bare hands. But like Stanley and Tony, there's a child-boy with not-so-nice instincts lurking under his polish, and Weiner is clear on where he stands when it comes to those instincts, particularly as they affect the lives of the women he has relationships with; in fact, the show offers some of the most explicitly pro-feminist narratives I've seen on television.

Among those is "Maidenform," an episode of *Mad Men* that begins from within the experience of women but concludes with an unexpected glimpse into the consciousness of a man, as he is challenged, perhaps for the first time in his life, to consider the effect of male dominance—which he has exercised throughout the episode—on women. It's one of the best, least tied-up-in-ribbons endings of any episode I've seen (right up there alongside the ambiguity of the final episode of *The Sopranos*) and made me want to write a fangirlish note to Matt Weiner. (I chickened out.)

On the surface, the episode is about the sexual objectification of women. It opens with short scenes of each one of the central women characters putting on the constricting bras and girdles of the era, making themselves presentable for the work day. But although Peggy is the only one of the creative team who actually wears a bra, she is excluded from a new campaign for *Playtex*. She's been assigned to the campaign, but her objections to the male-fantasy-inspired idea (lingerie that makes women into a Jackie Kennedy wife by day and Marilyn Monroe mistress by night) are ignored, she isn't informed about meetings, and the door is shut in her face at the audition for models. After the idea is sold, she isn't invited to the guys' celebration (at the Tom-Tom club, a stripper bar). Frustrated, she asks Joan how to get the men to take her seriously, and Joan advises that she "stop dressing like a little girl." So, she glams herself up and crashes the guys' celebration, where she giggles and submits cheerfully when one of the Playtex reps pulls her onto his lap. If playing *femme* is what's required to become a part of the team, she'll do it.

In another one of the episodes' story lines, Don and Betty attend a country club fashion show and auction, which features women in bathing suits (true to the era, no muscles and plenty of soft flesh). Leaving Betty at the show, Don sneaks off to see his mistress Bobbie Barrett, whose aggressively erotic talk annoys him, and he lets her know it. Then when she reveals that he has a reputation among the women of her set for being sexually proficient, he becomes furious and ties her to the bed; "I told you to stop talking" he says and storms off. Clearly, although he enjoys depersonalizing Bobbie while they are having sex (he tells her to stop talking several times), he doesn't like being treated like a sex toy himself. He may want a "Marilyn" for a mistress, but he wants a silent one. As for his wife, he married her because she was a "Jackie" and when, the next morning, he finds her serving cereal in a bikini that she bought at the auction, he doesn't like it and tells her so, leaving her puzzled and shamed. The duality of the new ad lives in Don's psyche.

The episode is one of the many *Mad Men* episodes, written by a man, that is strikingly attuned to the price women pay for male fantasies and ambivalences about women. (It might have been called "What do Men Want?") But instead of leaving Don unconscious about his need for control and the injustice of his expectations, the double binds it places his women in, Weiner gives Don a jolt of recognition. Don is shaving and his daughter Sally (Kiernan Shipka) is gazing up

FIGURE 13 What men want: Jackie by day, Marilyn by Night. "Maidenform" episode of *Mad Men*. Shown: Jon Hamm. AMC.

at him adoringly. "I'm not going to talk at all, Daddy" she says, because she doesn't want him to cut himself. Hearing this, Don's mood abruptly changes: he stops shaving, tells Sally to leave, and, shaken, sits down on the toilet. In one chilling moment, he's seen the budding, in his own daughter, of the subservience, the docility, that women learn men expect of them. The thought is what feminists used to call a click moment. Does he want his own daughter growing up silent and obedient to a man? As Don, sitting on the toilet, stares into space, the camera pulls back to reveal both Don and his troubled reflection in the mirror in the hall.

Not June Cleaver: From *Ally McBeal* to *Killing Eve*

Powerful women have never been that hard to find in the movies or on television. Often, however, they are the villainesses: the schemers, the man stealers, glammed up to the point of caricature, like Alexis Carrington. Others have been what Susan Douglas calls "bionic bimbos": their powers are of the super-human variety, and represent, according to Douglas, a "media compromise with feminism": "They would show us women with power, but in comic book settings that could never be mistaken for feminism." Some were compromises of other sorts: the Angels had guns and knew how to use them but at Charlie's bidding. These shows were entertaining and transgressive in some ways, but comfortably unrealistic. More earth-bound female characters who have fought for, owned, and acted on their power have come to us largely via cable and BBC: Jane Tennyson (Helen Mirren) of *Prime Suspect*, Carrie Mathieson (Claire Danes) of *Homeland*, the inmates of Litchfield in *Orange is the New Black*, Jackie (Edie Falco) of *Nurse Jackie*. Note however the price of being a fearless female, even on cable: Jane is an alcoholic with a crappy love-life, Carrie is bipolar and so driven by her work that by the final season she seems to have totally forgotten she has a child, Nurse Jackie is a drug addict, and the women of OITNB are . . . in prison. Still none of those characters are cutesy or silly or spend their days, like the women of *Sex and the City*, drinking cocktails or shopping for grossly overpriced shoes. And their issues are not gender dependent or gender coded; the men of cable are similarly fucked-up, and worse (e.g. *Dexter*, *Breaking Bad*). You don't find untarnished characters, male or female, on postmodern cable.

The networks are something else; the "one hand gives; the other takes away" phenomenon, with its wariness of giving offense to traditional viewers, remained the rule for much longer. In the background of resolving the tension between progress and tradition, always, is the fear of (a stereotype of) feminism. Women wielding guns is one thing: it's a genuflection to the iconography of male power; women bossing men around, competing with them in traditionally male professional domains is another; a challenge to the hierarchy of men on top, it's felt as castrating. Some shows—like *Prime Suspect*—have taken the problem head-on; a major theme of the first season is how Jane negotiates the scorn and derision of the men she works with, who chafe at having a female chief call the shots. The American versions—*The Closer* and its spin-off *Major Crimes*—gesture toward the tension, but are careful to feminize their female leads in compensation: Brenda Leigh Johnson (Kyra Sedgwick) has a honeyed Southern accent and quells her anxiety with candy that she keeps hidden in her top drawer; her successor, Sharon Raydor (Mary McDonnell), is soft-spoken and serene to the point of otherworldliness. Neither has the sharp edges of Jane Tennyson.

Ally McBeal's "Third Wave" Feminism

The courtroom and the hospital are familiar venues for prime-time television to bow to the comfortable division of labor: surgeon/nurse; lawyer/secretary. The familiar hierarchy reassures traditional viewers that all is in order in TV Land, even if women are marching for equal rights outside. So, what do you do when the lady is the litigator? One approach is to go explicitly "third wave"—or, to be more precise, a white girl version of the third wave, that goes out of its way to dis-identify with the hairy-legged puritanism of the foremothers rather than, as in women-of-color feminism, critiquing the centering of white women's issues and hero-ines. *Ally McBeal*, which ran from 1997 to 2002, is a great example. The show had nothing but scorn for the "second wave" that Mary Jo of *Designing Women* proudly asserted on her T-shirt and in her concluding speech to the Hill-Thom-as episode. Ally (Calista Flockhart) flirts with male clients without any thought to sexual harassment laws, and water-cooler talk with the men about penis size is not only OK, it's practically obligatory, to demonstrate that the heroines are not *those* kinds of feminists—you know, the kinds who don't wear makeup and can't take a joke. Frequently, those kinds of feminists are themselves the butt of jokes; for example, when Ally's roommate Renee (Lisa Nicole Carson, who of course being Black is portrayed as less uptight about everything, especially sexuality) tries to convince Ally there's nothing wrong with being attracted to a male model with a large penis, she points out that men are attracted to *her* "golden, lofty, globes." Ally: "But we're different . . . we have double standards to live up to." In another episode she sums her-self up: "I am a strong, working career girl who feels empty without a man—the National Organization for Women, they have a contract out on my head."

Stereotypes of second-wave feminism's attitudes aside, Ally's emptiness without a man didn't annoy me as much as her ridiculous self-description as "strong." Murphy Brown (or even Mary Jo from *Designing Women*) would roll her eyes. As a career girl, Ally is a mess who can't even hold her shit together at the sight of an attractive male. In fact, any kind of excitement makes Ally lose her cool. When she gets angry, she screeches like a little child having a temper tantrum. When she's upset, she sputters, stammers, and (as she so adorably admits) generally loses control over the English language. Often, her sexual attractions are represented through the magic of digital fantasy: Ally's tongue grows huge and hangs out at the sight of a young male client. But lest you think there's a full-grown, desiring woman inside that skinny kid prancing around in oversize pajamas, she hallucinates dancing babies, too.

FIGURE 14 Ally McBeal and her dancing baby. Shown: Callista Flockhart. Fox.

For some critics, Ally's dishevelment (and her immature Lolita body) was a "slap in the face of the real-life working girl" who makes "male power and female powerlessness seem harmless, cuddly, sexy, safe, and sellable."[7] For others, the show hits a "third-wave" cultural "nerve" in depicting the confusion and self-doubt that many women feel has been air-brushed out of the advertisements of the hyper-competent, ambitious working woman.[8] Still others bemoan the preoccupation with snagging a male that infects *Sex and the City*, too. For myself, the fact that David E. Kelley (creator and writer) expected us to find Ally's pouts and obliviousness to the world outside herself cute—as when she describes a rabbi's yarmulke as "that thingy on your head"!—was far more irritating than her preoccupation with various men. Sexual relationships dominated *The L Word*, too. But those women were hot babes, not pouting girl-children.

I watched and enjoyed Ally, even when I wanted to smash her face. But she belongs to another era. It's difficult to imagine anyone selling a show today in which male power and female powerlessness and/or incompetence are seen as cuddly or harmless. In 2016, the fatherly, feminist Obama was replaced by a man who not only thinks it's OK to grab women by the pussy but brags about it. His opponent was the most famous second-wave feminist in the world, and the election was one in which she had to contend not only with the same old stereotypes of her generation of feminists as shrill ideologues but new attacks from Bernie Sanders supporters who saw Clinton as a tool of Wall Street, an apologist for the establishment, and insufficiently committed to working-class problems.[9]

Interestingly, the most solid block of voters who resisted this picture were Black women. Unlike many of Sanders's young followers they were never going to buy the notion that there was little difference between Trump and Clinton. They knew who cared about protecting human rights and who was going to trample all over them. And they weren't so thin-skinned as white suburban women were about being tagged as bitchy or aggressive. It isn't surprising to me that it was a Black woman—Shonda Rhimes—who was the first prime-time writer to create competent, unapologetically ambitious female characters who aren't made to pay for speaking their minds or demanding their place in the world.

Conventional and Subversive: *Grey's Anatomy*

Unlike most viewers, I didn't get hooked on *Grey's Anatomy*, which premiered in 2005 and continues running today, until several seasons had passed. I thought it was going to be a generic hospital show, and I had seen just about every one of those from the most superficial (*Dr. Kildare*, *Ben Casey*, *Marcus Welby*, *MD*) to the quirkier ones that I loved (*St. Elsewhere* and *House*). In many ways, *Grey's Anatomy* is a conventional women's show, with story lines centered on romantic turmoil and ambivalence and located in a hospital that has a new crisis every week. During the first season, no doubt in an attempt to lure mass audiences, the opening credits featured a montage mixing shots of hospital equipment with a babe fixing her eyelashes, red high heels, champagne being poured, the back of a dress (not a hospital gown) being zipped, and legs entwined in a bed, while in the background a soft, femme-y song played. The first episode opens with Meredith Grey (Ellen Pompeo) waking up after a night of casual sex with McDreamy (Patrick Dempsey, who she doesn't know yet is a doctor at the hospital. The opening sequence alone suggested what was coming was going to be more of what we were used to.

But Rhimes makes these concessions to convention (which, after all, would not be reproduced so often if they weren't satisfying to female viewers) while subverting other expectations of the doctor show genre. *St. Elsewhere* had Denzel Washington (sadly, rarely featured); *ER* had Eriq Le Salle, a surly token surgeon. *Grey's* has a genuinely diverse cast, including a very short Black woman, a full-bodied Latina, and a dour-looking Asian. This may seem like a big yawn now, with HBO and Showtime regularly featuring Black performers and racially themed narratives, and CBS All Access's *The Good Fight* located in a Black law firm, but *Grey* broke what until then was the network mold: not everyone was drop-dead gorgeous and being non-white was unexceptional. The chief of surgery was a Black male (James Pickens Jr.)—and later, a Black female. The show was narrated by Meredith, whose friendship with another woman, Christina Yang (Sandra Oh, the dour Asian), developed over the course of the first season to be as central, if not more central, than her love life, as they became each other's "person"; not since Cagney and Lacey had viewers seen women who were as important to one another. Drawn to each other's cynicism and intelligence, Meredith and Christina both had romances with gorgeous doctors higher up on the food chain, but neither behaved like salivating nitwits at the sight of the (admittedly unusually good-looking) male staff. And I loved it that Miranda Bailey (Chandra Wilson)—the first genuinely ordinary-looking woman to have a top role on network TV—did not slide into the background, as I expected at first, but remained a central character (who got a top job and also got herself a gorgeous man, a departure from the stereotype of the chubby lovelorn woman).

Shonda Rhimes is an expert at combining the progressive (diverse cast, strong women) and the conventional (plots centered on love affairs or/and disasters) in just the right proportions to win a huge following while inserting subtly subversive feminist elements. I haven't followed her later productions, including the hugely popular *How to Get Away with Murder* that has Viola Davis as its lead. But by the second season of *Grey* I noticed that the tacky opening sequence and song were gone, and gradually, feminist issues began to creep into the plot lines. "Silent All These Years" (the episode's title is taken from the Tori Amos song), like the *Designing Women* Thomas-Hill show, was inspired by an actual hearing that had left women gasping over the triumph of sympathy and identification with an accused man over honoring a woman's story. However, the script doesn't take on the Kavanaugh hearing itself; instead, it's a kind of counternarrative, of a world in which women are not only believed, but treated with warmth, dignity, and tenderness. It's also about the high price of silence.

The story-line follows the aftermath of two rapes: one, a date rape that left Dr. Jo Karev's (Camilla Luddington) birthmother pregnant, the other a young woman named Abby (Khalilah Joi) who had been violently attacked and raped in an alley by a stranger. The two stories are woven together narratively by cutting back and forth between Jo's meeting with her birth mother and her caring for her patient at the hospital, and thematically by the contrast between Jo's birth mother, who is so broken by the rape that she only survives through decades of erasure and silence, and the young woman, who because of the delicate care that she receives from Jo and Dr. Teddy Altman (Kim Raver) is able to endure a rape kit and ultimately tell her husband about what happened. At the beginning of the episode, Abby wants neither the police nor her husband informed; like Jo's birth mother, she desires only to forget. But while Jo's mother, silent all these years, has been emotionally depersonalized in a way from which there is no return, and can't bear to even have Jo touch her hand, Abby in 2019, surrounded by other women who understand and empathize, is able to tentatively move forward.

Two scenes are key in establishing the difference between the trauma of rape for Jo's birth mother, ashamed and alone without anyone to confide in, and Abby's tentatively developing trust. At first unwilling to have a rape test done, when she eventually agrees, the show makes the bold decision to follow the procedure step-by-step, and each photo of her injuries, each swab of DNA, each contact with her bruised body, is orchestrated in the scene as the very opposite of the forced invasion that was the rape. Before each procedure in the protocol (informative in itself; I suspect few people know what a rape kit actually contains), she is asked if she is ready, and a "yes" is required before anything, no matter how minor, is done. It's a terrific scene, unsparingly revealing her injuries to the viewer, but equally attentive to depicting the tenderness with which Jo and Addison perform each procedure.

Later, in a solution to how to get Abby to the OR for a reparative operation without having to endure any man's gaze, the women of the hospital—doctors, nurses, orderlies, receptionists—line both sides of the hall she has to travel, so that all she sees are women—their expressions warm, sympathetic, but unstaring, as she is wheeled, slowly and gently toward the elevator. Like *Designing Women*, it's a fantasy world composed entirely of women—a world that offers something no Marcus Welby or McDreamy can supply: when one's body and heart have been ripped apart, the other women get it. My first idol movie critic Pauline Kael would probably sneer at such a fantasy, but it had the

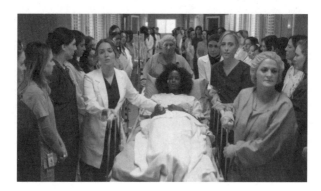

FIGURE 15 "Silent All these Years"; Shonda Rhimes, inspired by #MeToo, tackles rape. Principles shown: Camilla Luddington, Khalilah Joi, Kim Raver et al., *Grey's Anatomy*. ABC.

cultural critic in me, the writer who recoils when a point is made in a forced, overly "political" manner, weeping into my kettle-corn.

Post-Trump Feminism: *The Good Fight*

Shows of sisterhood can go too far, though. I cringed when a more recent show—*Tommy*, in which Edie Falco plays Abigail Thomas, the newly appointed police chief of Los Angeles—indulged in a shameless "I am Spartacus" moment and had a half dozen of the women in the courtroom stand up when the defendant in a murder case (she claimed she'd been sexually assaulted by the man she killed) was asked to "Please rise." There's a line between emotionally resonant dramatics (as in "Silent All These Years") and pandering descent into clichés of female solidarity. *Tommy* also goes out of its way to check all the boxes: in the very first episode we learn that Tommy is gay, has a biracial daughter (in a former life, she had been married to a Black man), and although no-nonsense and no-frills, has a very warm heart and offers to take home an immigrant child in danger of deportation. She is also a rape survivor who had been disbelieved (the rapist was a high-ranking cop), and many suspect that she has been hired (to replace a chief accused of serial harassment) only because she is a woman. She feels the burden of that suspicion acutely: "If I fail it will be twenty years before they give another woman this job." Yawn.

After this shower of clichés, it's important for the show to reassure viewers that Tommy isn't part of some coven. She describes herself ruefully as having become a feminist icon when she lost her own rape suit (I mean, who wants to be worshipped by thousands of women?); "I'd rather have the ten years of my career back" she says. Later, the show takes an equally sarcastic poke at feminism when another character refers to Tommy as the "Feminist savior of the LAPD." OK, so despite her other credentials (and Edie Falco's truly impressive lesbian police chief stride) we know Tommy isn't *that* kind of feminist—you know, the political kind—but the kind that disdains labels.

The feminism of *The Good Fight*, another post-Trump-election show and a spin-off from the successful *The Good Wife*, is more complicated. Diane Lockhart (Christine Baranski) neither disowns second-wave feminist politics (as in *Ally McBeal*) nor exploits its tropes of sisterhood (as in the Spartacus moment in *Tommy*) but shows just how much more complex we are than as painted by the stereotypes—whether they come from the Right *or* the Left. We know, from *The Good Wife*, that Diane is a supporter of Emily's List. But in *The Good Fight*, even the best fight has a downside. In the fourth season's opening episode (paralleling the opening episode of the first season, in which Trump is inaugurated) Diane, temporarily blacked out, has a dream in which Hillary is POTUS. She's dumbfounded but delighted—until she realizes that in this alternative reality, #MeToo doesn't exist and Harvey Weinstein is doing his stuff unimpeded. "I'm not sure I like this world," she is dismayed to realize. But don't leap to the conclusion that she's an advocate of zero tolerance! "People who make history and do good are complicated," she says in another episode, not so much in defense of the behavior of the firm's founder, who had sexually exploited his secretary and stenographer for years, as against the politics of purity, whether evangelical or left-leaning. In another episode, when a progressive young woman who runs a website called Assholes to Avoid berates her (and her entire generation of feminists) for being too soft on men, she replies, "You know what your trouble is? You think women can only be one thing."

Diane, on the other hand, is many things: glamorously long-legged in her absurdly glittery power suits—hard to believe a real lawyer would dress as if going to a Broadway opening—but good-natured and tolerant in her relationships. Neither shrill nor silent, she likes to laugh—but she's also often the adult in the room, quietly thoughtful when discussion deteriorates into squabbling. She despises Trump and for a while, disgusted by the fragmented, ideological chaos of Democrats, participates in an all-female radical resistance group. She's unwilling to follow them, however, when they propose mucking around with voting machines. She's open about her own feminist politics but married to a Republican ballistics expert (Gary Cole). All of this struck a chord with me, a second waver who twenty years ago startled the men in my classes when they discovered I wasn't the humorless, puritanistic man-hater they expected. Twenty years later, I was excoriated by other feminists on Facebook for criticizing a zero-tolerance policy and insisting that Al Franken's and Donald Trump's behavior with women were far from comparable.

The other women are complicated, too. They all have romantic lives, but it's the characters' brains rather than their relationships that are highlighted. From named partners Diana Lockhart and Liz Reddick (Audra McDonald), to associates Lucca Quinn (Cash Jumbo) and Maia Rindell (Rose Leslie), to aspiring investigator Melissa Gold (Sarah Steele)—the women at the firm are really, really smart. None of them neatly satisfies any gendered or racial stereotypes, which is in keeping with the show's refusal to partake in white liberal self-congratulation even as it relentlessly skewers Trumpism. Melissa is the most recognizable in her feminism, the one most insistent on believing the woman in a rape suit; but she has no problem becoming the adviser to a GOP colleague trying for a judgeship. The law firm that Diane joins at the beginning of the first season is not the ethnic rainbow of *Grey's Anatomy*; it's a Black firm, and Diane is the only white partner, often the only one in the room when the power players are together, a turning of the usual tables that exposes the ideal of token diversity as another vestige of white-centered TV culture. But race, like gender, doesn't define the characters evenly or predictably. Lucca, unlike some of her more overtly political colleagues, isn't willing to make everything about race; however, she is also the one to point out that only the Black members of the firm know the names of Black victims of violence. (The next scene shows the white lawyers trying to memorize them; "Let's see . . . Eric Gardner, Tamir Rice, Michael Brown . . .") None of the women—or the men, for that matter—are only one thing.

What makes *The Good Fight* more of a show for our times than *Tommy*, however, isn't its more subtle, layered character portraits or its explicit taking on of contemporary issues (which *Tommy* does too) but its focus on the disorientation—the damage done to our sense of reality—caused by the three years of legal, moral, and epistemological chaos we have suffered since Trump's election. It's often remarked, as I noted earlier, that the Trump presidency is a reality show. But although we

FIGURE 16 Tables turned in *The Good Fight*. Principles shown: Christine Baranski, Delroy Lindo, Cush Jumbo. CBS All Access.

know reality shows are faked, they also follow fairly predictable conventions, whereas the Trump Show has defied all our expectations of what can and can't happen. "The guardrails are off and I can't see the road," says Diane's husband Kurt, who voted Republican but becomes more and more distressed by Trumpism. Nothing could be truer. The guardrails (the law, the constitution, the separation of powers) truly do seem to have come off, and it's been a hugely disorienting shock to all of us who learned in grade school that although evil men can flourish anywhere, our democracy has protections against things falling entirely apart. The informative part of TV's split personality, however, rarely mirrors that shock, as pundits who have been trained to remain calm and equanimous, their psyches seemingly intact as they cover a POTUS who is dangerously incompetent in every way, daily announce the most dreadful events.

So, it's left to the fictional side of television to adequately represent our reality—which ironically doesn't feel like reality anymore at all. Not reality as we've known it, that is. *The Good Fight* announces this right away, but in startling (and gorgeous) opening credits that may have some viewers puzzled at first. One by one, in a dramatically filmed series of sequences, ironically accompanied by a courtly Baroque soundtrack more fitting of a *Masterpiece Theatre* series about Elizabeth I, the accessories that we might find in any woman lawyer's office (at least, as represented on television)—law books, high heels, fashionable briefcases, cut-glass decanters of liquor, office phones—are exploded to bits, leaving behind the debris of bourgeois professionalism.

The Good Fight, as we soon find out, will make the "everything is in disarray" nature of life under Trumpian rule—the "What the fuck is going on?" aspect—a central theme. Fake Twitter accounts, fake news, and cyber terrorism feature prominently, and it becomes harder and harder to tell who is doing what and for what reason. In season three, Lucca interviews a woman who may or may not be Melania Trump and who is interested in acquiring the so-called pee tapes; Lucca decides she is a fake, but the viewer is left unsure. In season one, Felix Staples (John Cameron Mitchell), an alt-right gadfly who has participated in a cyber plot aimed at the fun of disruption, is aghast to find out his partner in crime is a Bernie Bro set on social

FIGURES 17 AND 18 *The Good Fight's* opening credits: "The world as we knew it in free fall." CBS All Access.

revolution. Later, Diane and managing partner of the firm, Adrian Boseman (Delroy Lindo), muse together on the roof of their building, surveying a blacked-out Chicago. "It's a grim time out there," Adrian remarks. Diane adds: "Weird." Adrian: "Something feels like it's come detached, like a piece of machinery that doesn't sound right." It's one of many times that the characters express their disorientation openly.

In the second season, after a rash of murders of lawyers, Diane begins microdosing psilocybin to help cope with her sense of impending doom. But when she confides to Liz that she often worries she is going insane, it's not clear to the viewer whether drugs or her mental state are causing hallucinations or whether, for example, there really was a couple dancing in the building across the way wearing Trump masks. When Diane finds blonde hairs on Kurt's jacket, they turn out to belong not to another woman, but Eric Trump, who has worn Kurt's jacket at a shooting range. Later, Kurt, who has been hired by the Trump boys to take them on safari, is injured when one of them accidentally shoots him. Surreal? Yes, but no more so than the fact that the sons of our POTUS have posted Instagram pics with their trophies of dead endangered species. In the third and fourth seasons, we are introduced to flamboyant Roland Blum (Michael Sheen), a disciple of Roy Cohn who articulates the Fox/Trump doctrine of making the evidence support your story rather than the other way around. "Who needs the truth when you're winning?" he explains to Maia, "There is beauty in a well-told lie." Blum, who instructs Maia never to deny, explain, or apologize, is so eccentric that he could easily be a character from a Gore Vidal or Terry Southern satire. But, as Diane remarks, this weird world that we are living is one in which "what starts out as satire quickly becomes the real thing."

Is It a Thriller? Is It a Comedy? Is It a Fashion Show? No, It's *Killing Eve*

This weird world has unleashed a lot of creativity, too. With the social and legal guardrails off, what's to stop us from turning the absence of protective rules into an opportunity to put our super egos to bed in our art? That's a big part of the addictive appeal of *Killing Eve*. *Killing Eve* is hardly the first show to feature a psychopathic killer as a central character. But what we typically enjoy about these characters is the chill of pure evil, like Hannibal Lecter, who savors a fine chianti and fava beans along with human body parts. Supposedly, psychopaths can be quite charming when they want to be—it's how they ensnare their victims—but it's hard to think of a fictional psychopath who charms the *viewer*. Our one lovable killer, *Dexter*, doesn't count, as he has the redeeming feature of having been taught by his father to channel his psychopathy into killing only bad guys. The show never goes *beyond* good and evil; it's about the struggle *between* good and evil.

Killing Eve does go beyond—*everything*: genre, recognizable politics, sexual stereotypes, conventional notions about love and sex, and even what counts as a fashionable outfit. Villanelle, the female assassin (Jodie Comer), may be evil—but she's also whimsical, undefinable, and irresistible, and much of the pleasure of the show comes simply from watching her: her ever-changing facial expressions (giggling or pouting like a five-year-old one moment, coldly eyeing her next victim in another), her clothing (sometimes fashionably butch, sometimes as pink and poufy as a little girl at a beauty pageant, other times like a little boy who couldn't care less, sometimes simply bizarre), her unpredictable moves and moods. It's impossible to figure her out. Did she kill the boy in the hospital bed next to hers on impulse, to steal his stickers, or as an act of euthanasia? Does she herself even know? Whatever; she looks far more fetching loping down the street, her tummy very slightly chubby in his Target boy sleepwear, than Ally McBeal did prancing around in her oversized pajamas with the little sheep on them. We can almost forgive the fact that she is a sadistic murderer because she gives us so much pleasure with her fashion choices, and they give her so much pleasure, too. (In order to escape from the hospital, she has to put on a nurse's dowdy slippers; she can barely force herself to do it.)

It's fairly easy to understand the magnetic pull she exerts over Eve (Sandra Oh), who discovers that she needs doses of danger to keep her heart beating, but what's the nature of Villanelle's attraction to Eve? It's sexual but not primarily, it's not about Eve's great, big hair (which Villanelle does love), and it's not just admiration—although it's clear Villanelle does admire something in Eve that other people lack. But what is it? Villanelle may be a trickster, but Eve is just . . . unfathomable. She seems normal in many ways, but it's a foggy sort of normal, a walking sleep that only Villanelle

FIGURE 19 Mad love? Bad romance? Sandra Oh and Jodie Comer in *Killing Eve*. BBC America/AMC.

is able to wake her out of. And even when awake, she seems not to know what she's doing with herself half the time, even as she has an instinctive brilliance for investigation. Eve and Villanelle seem to be in love with each other (which causes them to "do crazy things"—as Villanelle says—like try to kill each other) but to make those words "in love" apply, they need to be reinvested with something that isn't within my vocabulary—and certainly isn't found in the conventions of romantic/sexual relationships, depicted in movies and TV, even the kinkier ones.

Some reviewers have tried to slot *Killing Eve* within recognizable, if transgressive, categories: Melanie McFarland, in *Salon*, describes it as a "feminist thriller" for the era of

#MeToo, that "slakes one's desire to see piggish misogynists get what's coming to them"[10] by having them dispatched cold-bloodedly by the disarmingly pretty and seductive Villanelle while complicating the simplicity of sisterhood by making her as dangerous to the woman she's irresistibly drawn to—Eve—as to the men she disdains. Along those lines, Willa Paskin in *Slate* writes that the show warns the viewer that underestimating women is dangerous.[11] They may appear, as Villanelle frequently does, as hyperfeminine; but her hairpin is a deadly weapon.

But Villanelle isn't your typical *femme fatale*. Her emotional life is more like that of a child. She likes to play, to goof around. She is drawn to toys, then throws them away carelessly. At one point, after murdering its mother, she picks up a baby and seems to take genuine delight in playing with it. But she soon tires of it, is annoyed by its crying, and when Dasha Duzren (Harriet Walter), Villanelle's former trainer and mentor, dumps the baby in a nearby trash can, she indifferently walks away. The scene is both shocking and darkly funny and reprises a similar sequence of events that takes place when we are first introduced to Villanelle, in an outdoor café, where she is staring at a little girl eating ice cream and smiling at her mother. Wanting to catch the little girl's attention, Villanelle works at copying her smile, and it isn't clear whether this is someone with an absence of human emotion trying to fake it or she's just awkwardly being friendly. The little girl is wary at first—why is this stranger smiling at me?—but eventually smiles back and is rewarded by having her ice cream dumped onto her dress. The scene is a perfect introduction for a character who will always keep us off balance, and a feminist message seems forced and irrelevant to either her, Eve, or their relationship with each other. They are profoundly strange people, the show is "hilarious, bloody, [and] unclassifiable,"[12] and it's enough that it's so enjoyable to watch.

EPILOGUE: JULY 4, 2020

In an episode of *The Good Fight*, the sky suddenly erupts with huge, circular balls of lightening that no one has ever seen before; the lightning balls set fire to several buildings. Mesmerized, one character muses that it must be the "beginning of end times." Lucca, who in another episode has been arrested for mothering while black, is more jaded about bizarre, scary occurrences: "One more thing to worry about," she sighs. Looking back at the episode now, it's hard for me to not see the episode as a an inchoately brilliant metaphor for the inevitability that Trumpian chaos would unleash a karmic disaster that would pay us all back for being so stupid as to elect him, and possibly, might bring him down at the same time.

Thanks in no small part to television, Trump rose to a position of prominence that would have been unimaginable a few decades ago. Not even Ronald Reagan had gone straight from TV (and in Reagan's case, movies) to the White House. And Trump wasn't even a successful actor, but a failing businessman when *The Apprentice* saved him. That performance, and a lot of self-promotion, managed to convince a significant number of voters that he would be an able leader of the country. Once installed in the Oval Office, the pretense at competence was harder for Trump to sustain. But with the help of Mitch McConnell, William Barr, a bunch of genuflecting Republican politicians, and a devoted base that adores him no matter what he does, he managed.

The mainstream media, unprepared to cope with a habitually lying POTUS or Trump's extremes of racism, sexism, and xenophobia, helped sustain the illusion that, despite all evidence to the contrary, this was still a normal—if reprehensible—presidency, attained in a normal election, and sustained by normal means. It wasn't so much what they said but how they said it. The most horrific things were being done—from children in cages to multiple violations of the constitution—but the viewer-calming conventions of liberal broadcasting and its commitment to balance prevented any outright displays of what so many of us were feeling: How can it be that this is our president? How can it be that he's lasted for so long? Increasingly, watching the Trump Show, despite the pundits' branding, was not like watching a reality show but a *surreality* show. And the dissonance between what many of us were feeling and the illusion of normalcy that the mainstream media projected, simply by remaining so professional about it all, made it all the more surreal.

Today, any pretense that Trump's presidency lives within any boundaries of the normal have been shattered by Trump's lethally inept mishandling of a raging pandemic and his doubling-down against a (belated) national protest against the legacy and practices of systemic racism. As in the opening credits of *The Good Fight*, an (overdue) explosion has taken place, leaving us surrounded by debris. For broadcast news, the tipping point may have been the evening that Trump took the opportunity to tear-gas a peaceful protest in order to walk unobstructed to the spot he had chosen to stage an absurd photo op.[1] He wanted to displace the narrative that he had huddled in a basement bunker during the protests— something that actually needed no justification (we try to protect our presidents), but which, in the world according to Donald Trump, was an intolerably unmanly image. So, flanked by flunkies and Secret Service, he strode across the street that the National Guard had cleared with gas and rubber bullets, cutting through the protesters (as Trump later described it) "like butter." Garrett Haake, on the scene for MSNBC, abandoned all pretense at neutrality, aghast at what he'd just seen. "The protest was entirely peaceful!!!" he kept repeating; like John Chancellor at Little Rock, he couldn't believe what he had seen. Neither could viewers, still reeling from the sight of that brutal knee on George Floyd's neck, impervious to his cries of "I can't breathe" and the absence of a pulse. Floyd was one in a long line of Black men—and some women—to be killed without provocation by the police. But a bystander's video had captured the killing in such wrenching, minute-by-minute, intimate detail (he called for his mother as he died) that white obliviousness broke apart in an unprecedented way. This was *real* reality television, even more jolting than those broadcast images from the integration of Little Rock's Central High that I discussed at the beginning of this book. And now, alongside that raw and haunting image was this other one, entirely staged and in its own way as grotesque as the other: Donald Trump in front of St. John's church, stiff and grim (I think he meant to seem resolute), an upside-down Bible being brandished, as Kamala Harris put it, "like a Trump steak,"[2] while the smell of tear gas still lingered in the air.

By the night of Trump's photo op, the illusion of normalcy was already faltering, challenged by a pandemic that had fallen on us like those balls of lightening raining down on Chicago in *The Good Fight*. Many of us watched the protests

FIGURE 20 Trump blasts through peaceful protest against murder of George Floyd "like butter." The Hill.

FIGURE 21 This surreal photo-shoot may have been a tipping-point for news commentators C-SPAN.

sheltered in place, trying to be safe from the invasion of COVID-19, an elusive new viral danger that Trump appeared to be as oblivious to as the humanity of, well, everyone but himself. When the numbers finally forced him to admit it wasn't merely another Democratic hoax perpetuated by the fake news, he turned daily televised briefings—surrounded by worried-looking scientists unsure how to represent reality without humiliating the president or/and getting fired—into opportunities to minimize the danger ("No big deal; it'll be gone in the spring") and promote untested and dangerous cures. He mocked those who weren't manly enough to go without a mask and urged citizens to be brave "warriors" and risk infection for the good of the economy (while he and those close to him are tested every day). Ultimately, he abandoned the briefings and just let the virus do its thing as states opened up willy-nilly, their citizens' fates determined by whether they were led by cautious, science-respecting governors or those who followed the Edicts of Trump. With no national leadership, every rumor, every bit of speculation, every fragment of partial data, like the particles of viral protein themselves, has had its way with us—particularly those without access to health care, and communities of color, many of whom worked in essential, virus-friendly jobs.

It wasn't surprising to me when I asked my Facebook friends how their television habits had changed during the pandemic, that many of them had begun to avoid the news completely. Many feel it's for the sake of their mental health; they were overtaken with anxiety and "not their best selves" on a diet of pandemic information. Instead, they turned to Netflix and Hulu for binge-worthy series, perhaps tuning in once a day to Andrew Cuomo's demonstrations of actual leadership, as he managed to be both honest and comforting for the citizens of New York. For those of us who still kept up with the news compulsively, it now came to us from the living rooms, kitchens, and libraries of reporters and pundits—and exhausted doctors and nurses, trying to convey to viewers the scope of the disaster that Trump assured us would magically disappear one day—"and very soon." I became fascinated by the different settings of the at-home broadcasts: the huge, stunning homes one would happily shelter in place in *for a vacation*, the unbelievably immaculate, white kitchens that no virus would dare invade, staged as if for a realtor's showing, the "look at all my books" backdrops (you can actually read the titles of many of Eddie Glaude's, displayed as if on a Barnes and Noble shelf). And there was the virtual town hall, which reminded us that despite the surreality of life, there were still going to be primaries and a November election.

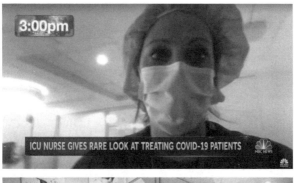

FIGURE 22 A–D Pandemic TV: inside besieged hospitals and celebrity homes. NBC News, MSNBC, YouTube, MSNBC.

FIGURE 22 A–D (Continued).

TV is keeping us company during this pandemic (present tense, as of this writing). But news broadcasters, finally, are less and less willing to maintain their smiling professional demeanor in the face of Trump's craven political maneuvering, the blind attachment on the part of his base, and what seems more and more like a desperate attempt to con his followers into seeing him as the leader of an escalating culture war—or perhaps even a new Civil War against "the radical left, the Marxists, the anarchists, the agitators [and]the looters." Yesterday, at Mount Rushmore (itself a deliberately provocative statement—the faces of American presidents are carved from rocks sacred to the Lakota people), he advertised himself as a courageous preserver of a sacred, truly *American* legacy, battling a "new far-left fascism" attempting "to wipe out our history, defame our heroes, erase our values and indoctrinate our children. Angry mobs are trying to tear down statues of our founders, deface our most sacred memorials and unleash a wave of violent crime in our cities."[3]

Are we at a tipping point (or "inflection point," as is now the fashion to say)? A line from *I Claudius* keeps coming to mind: "Let all the poisons hatch from the mud!" That does seem fitting. But who knows what's coming? Our failure to contain COVID-19 feels apocalyptic. But white America's overdue reckoning with the pandemic of racism brings hope of a new beginning.

As someone in the elderly category I admire those of my age who have joined the protests, but I don't have the courage to do so myself. I watch on television, wondering how I can contribute without getting sick and dying. As with everyone else, the anxiety is taking a toll on me. I nap in the daytime more than I used to, eat more sugary stuff and drink more coffee than I should. I worry a lot about my daughter, who has a job caring for horses that takes her out into the dangerous world outside our house twice a day. I wipe things down a lot. I'm giving my eyes a rest from mascara, and my hair is longer than it has been since the sixties. I talk on the telephone with my sisters, best friend, and therapist, and am grateful to have a spacious house to shelter in, Facebook friends to converse with and this book to write. (What will I do once I'm finished with it?) At night, post-Netflix or Lawrence O'Donnell, I snuggle under the covers with my dog Sean nestled against my back or curled up around my head like a furry hat and listen for hours to Stephen Sondheim until he's banished the demons and I fall asleep. I'm rarely able, as I used to regularly, to drift off with the TV on and the news in the background.

Susan Bordo
July, 2020

ACKNOWLEDGMENTS

ast July, I had just retired and was looking forward to having a blank slate before me, existentially as well as on my computer. So naturally, I had a meltdown. Preoccupied with bizarre symptoms (I break down nineteenth-century style) and a totally unexpected depression, I had completely forgotten that months before, I had submitted a proposal to Bloomsbury's "Object Lessons" series. Like a good deal of my work over the decades, it dealt with culturally created imagery and mythology and their challenge to our sense of reality, history, and truth. I called it "In Plato's Cave" and was told, very nicely (and accurately) that it didn't really work for the series. A few days later, I got another letter, this one from Christopher Schaberg, one of the series' editors: "Here's a crazy idea," he wrote, "what if we called this book *TV* or *Television*—and you could tell this story about truth, lying, pseudo-events, and reality by way of these different televisual moments/flash points?" Hell, yes, I thought, I'd much rather do that anyway—among other things, it would give me an excuse to watch a lot of shows.

The writing of the new proposal was very much a collaborative effort between me and Christopher, to whom I owe huge thanks for great suggestions and encouragement every step of the way. Then, through Facebook I found another collaborator: photographer and photo editor Rachel Youdelman, who researched historical images, prepared screen shots, and made invaluable suggestions about what illustrations to include. Rachel was indispensable; I had only to mention an episode or genre of still, and within a day or so, a collection of perfect images and background information would arrive in my email. Thanks also to my Facebook friends, who I queried regularly about their viewing habits and early memories and who provided the only real community I had— and a very warm, supportive one it was--during these months of isolation, my Research Assistant Ashe Cornelius, who zoomed through internet highways as I'll never be able to do, my agent Sam Stoloff, my friends Virginia Blum and Medford Moreland, and my family—Edward Lee, Cassie Lee, Binnie Klein, Scott Shapleigh, and Marilyn Silverman—for helping me through my crash, for sharing their own ideas and feelings, and for loving me no matter how much patience was required.

As bizarre and frightening that these past months have been for all of us, they actually turned out to be a perfect time to be working on the last chapters of this book; I feel very lucky to have had precisely this project during a time when bingeing on TV was not a guilty pleasure (actually, I've never felt very guilty about it) but essential to my work—and totally safe!

NOTES

Preface

1 Jeff Kisseloff, *The Box: An Oral History of Television 1920–1961* (Golden, CO: ReAnimus Press, 2013,1995), 109.

Chapter 1

1 "American Rhetoric: Top 100 Speeches," McCarthy-Welch Exchange, https://www.americanrhetoric.com/speeches/wel ch-mccarthy.html.

2 See "Please Mr. Prosecutor Mueller," in Susan Bordo, *Imagine Bernie Sanders as a Woman and other Writings on Politics and Media 2016–2019* (Denver, CO: Outskirts Press, 2020), 35–43.

Chapter 3

1 David Halberstam, *The Fifties* (New York: Fawcett Columbine, 1993), 508–20.

2 Gary Edgerton, *The Columbia History of American Television*, (New York: Columbia University Press, 2007), 264.

3 Ibid., 265.

4 As quoted in Ibid.

5 Halberstam, *The Fifties*, 675.

6 Frank was more interested in the drama than the service to social justice. As Gerald Green, then editor of *The Today Show* explains it: "The whole dispute in TV news back then was talking heads" versus "head-cracking….We used to sit in that screening room with Lodge and Reuven Frank, 'Look, they're beating somebody up. Get a minute of it!'" (Kisseloff, *The Box*, 348.)

7 Kisseloff, *The Box*, 366.

8 Ibid., 407.

9 Steven Stark, *Glued to the Set* (New York: Simon and Schuster, 1997), 52–6.

10 Susan Douglas, *Where the Girls Are: Growing Up Female with the Mass Media* (New York: Random House, 1994), 32.

11 Kisseloff, *The Box*, 334.

12 Ibid., 335.

13 Ibid., 332.

14 Ibid., 333–4.

15 David Zurawik, *The Jews of Prime Time* (Lebanon, PA: Brandeis University Press, 2003), 7.

16 Ibid., 17–47.

17 Matt Zoller Seitz, *Mad Men Carousel: The Complete Critical Companion* (New York: Abrams Press, 2017) 25–32.

Chapter 4

1 Daniel Boorstin, *The Image* (New York: Vintage, 1961), 36.

2 "The Best Historical Dramas to Binge," *TV Guide*, April 28, 2020, https://www.tvguide.com/news/best-historical-dramas-to-binge-watch-on-netflix-right-now/.

3 Roger Ailes, *You Are the Message* (New York: Doubleday, 1988), 15.

4 Gabriel Sherman, *The Loudest Voice in the Room* (New York: Random House, 2017), 187.

5 Ibid., 105.

6 Donald J. Trump, *The Art of the Deal* (New York: Random House, 1987), 57–8.

7 Chris Cillizza, "Kellyanne Conway offers alternative fact to explain why Trump isn't lying," CNN Politics, July 24, 2017, https://www.cnn.com/2017/07/24/politics/kellyanne-conway-trump/index.html.

8 Sheila Jasanoff, "The Eye of Everyman: Witnessing DNA in the Simpson Trial," *Social Studies of Science* 28, no. 5/6, (Oct.–Dec. 1998): 713–40.

9 Lawrence Schiller and James Willworth, *American Tragedy* (New York: Random House, 1996), 329–31.

10 Stark, *Glued to the Set*, 188–90.

11 Marie Brenner, "American Nightmare: The Ballad of Richard Jewell," *Vanity Fair*, February 1997, https://archive.vanityfair.com/article/share/1fd2d7ae-10d8-474b-9bf1-d1558af697be/.

12 Ronald J. Ostrow, "Richard Jewell Case Study," Columbia University, June 2000, www.columbia.edu/.../j6075/edit/readings/jewell.html.

13 "Eric Rudolph," https://en.wikipedia.org/wiki/Eric_Rudolph.

14 Cal Thomas, "Rumors, hyperbole seeped into news," *Lexington Herald Leader*, September 30, 2005, A13.

15 Jeanne Meserve and Aaron Brown, *CNN Reports,* September 29, 2005, from author's notes.

16 Thomas, "Rumors."

17 Mary Elizabeth Williams, "Hillary powers through pneumonia," *Salon*, September 12, 2016. https://www.salon.com/2016/09/12/hillary-powers-through-pneumonia-because-thats-what-women-do/.

18 Alex Seitz-Wald, Monica Alba, Andrea Mitchell, Kristen Welker, Kasie Hunt, "Clinton's Health Scare: Nine Unanswered Questions," *NBC News*, September 12, 2016, https://www.nbcnews.com/politics/2016-election/hillary-clinton-s-health-scare-9-unanswered-questions-n646551.

19 Jen Gunter, "I'm a doctor and these are the things I find concerning with Trump's medical letter," August 16, 2016, www.drjengunter.wordpress.com/2016/08/16.

20 Matthew Yglesias, "The real Clinton email scandal is that a bullshit story has dominated the campaign," *Vox*, November 4, 2016, http://www.vox.com/policy-and-politics/2016/11/4/13500018/clinton-email-scandal-bullshit.

21 See Susan Bordo, *The Destruction of Hillary Clinton: Untangling the Political Forces, Media Culture, and Assault on Fact that Decided the 2016 Election* (New York: Melville House, 2017) for full coverage and analysis of the various representations and scandals that plagued Clinton's candidacy.

Chapter 5

1 Ralph Keyes, *The Courage to Write* (New York: Henry Holt, 2003).

2 George Orwell, "Politics and the English Language," https://www.orwell.ru/library/essays/politics/english/e_polit.

3 Simone de Beauvoir, *The Second Sex* (New York: Alfred A. Knopf, 1957), esp. xv–xxx.

4 Kisseloff, *The* Box, 375.

5 Lara Bazelon, "Kamala Harris's Criminal Justice Record Killed Her Presidential Run," *The Appeal*, December 4, 2019, https://theappeal.org/kamala-harris-criminal-justice-record-killed-her-presidential-run/.

6 Natasha Korecki, Christopher Cadelago, and Marc Caputo, "'She had no remorse': Why Kamala Harris isn't a lock for VP," *Politico*, July 27, 2020.

Chapter 6

1 James Poniewozik, *Audience of One: Donald Trump, Television, and the Fracturing of America* (New York: Liverwright, 2019), 126–7.

2 Michael Kranish and Marc Fisher, *Trump Revealed* (New York: Scribner, 2016), 214.

3 Ibid., 215.

4 See *The Real Housewives Tell It Like It Is* ((Bravo Media, 2011) and Martha O'Connor, *The Real Housewives Get Personal* (Bravo Media, 2010).

5 Susan Herbst, *Rude Democracy: Civility and Incivility in American Politics* (Philadelphia: Temple University Press, 2010), 133.

6   Laura Stepp, "Mean Girls Myth," *Huffington Post*, February 23, 2011. https://www.huffpost.com/entry/mean-girls-myth_b_8 25800?guccounter=1&guce_referrer=aHR0cDovL3d3dy5ia W5nLmNvbS9zZWFyY2g_cT1NRUFOJTIwR0lSTFMlM jBNWVRIJkZPUk09QVRVUjAxJlBDPUFUVVImUFRBR z1BVFVSMDdSQU5E&guce_referrer_sig=AQAAAEvUjy-FdiLLSNJUUc8gtpcMYeJQnKnVe1ugYp_lrvp5t3FtARQA qfHTmxZhUYLpBRnpvtphISa5zGtFXw2bJ2gfjSBg6-MNb fQ9sAT88OuvVWQl2pgSj7hczSEmt_gUBr5XBfBGU7Mfqz F37GuoK19zZJgv1vfmlogZWA2oPkLY.

7   David Denby, *Snark* (New York: Simon and Schuster, 2009),

8   Kisseloff, *The Box*, 349.

9   Douglas, *Where the Girls Are*, 285.

10 Bonnie Dow, *Prime-Time Feminism* (Philadelphia: University of Pennsylvania Press, 1996), 138.

11 Ibid, 125.

12 Hearing of the Senate Judiciary Committee on the Nomination of Clarence Thomas to the Supreme Court, September 13, 2013, Electronic Text Center, University of Virginia Library, October 11, 1991.

13 Kavanaugh Hearing: Transcript, *Washington Post*, September 17, 2018.

Chapter 7

1   Susan Bordo, *The Male Body: A New Look at Men in Public and in Private* (New York: Farrar Straus and Giroux, 1999), 135.

2   David Chase, *The Sopranos: Selected Scripts from Three Seasons* (New York: Warner Books, 2002), 79.

3 Matt Zoller Seitz and Alan Sepinwall, *The Soprano Sessions* (New York: Abrams, 2019), 334.

4 Ibid., 31–2.

5 Ibid., 335.

6 David Bianculli, *The Platinum Age of Television* (New York: Anchor Books, 2017), 472.

7 Michelle Hammers, "Cautionary Tales of Liberation and Female Professionalism: The Case against Ally McBeal," *Western Journal of Communication* 69, no. 2 (2005): 167.

8 Leslie Heywood, "Hitting a Cultural Nerve: Another Season of Ally McBeal," *The Chronicle of Higher Education*, September 4, 1998.

9 Bordo, *The Destruction of Hillary Clinton*. See esp. 43–73.

10 Melanie McFarland, "Feminist thriller *Killing Eve* has proven a perfect show for the #MeToo era," *Salon*, May 26, 2018, https://www.salon.com/2018/05/26/feminist-thriller-killing-eve-has-proven-a-perfect-show-for-the-metoo-era/.

11 Willa Paskin, "*Killing Eve* Makes Murder Dangerously Fun," *Slate*, April 10, 2018, https://slate.com/culture/2018/04/bbc-americas-killing-eve-reviewed.html.

12 Jenna Scherer, "*Killing Eve*: The Cracked Female Spy-Thriller Buddy Comedy of the Year," *Rolling Stone*, May 14, 2018, https://www.rollingstone.com/tv/tv-news/killing-eve-the-cracked-female-spy-thriller-buddy-comedy-of-the-year-627960/.

Epilogue

1 Kamala Harris, "Trump Just Tear-Gassed Peaceful Protesters for A Photo-Op," Guardians of Democracy, https://theguar

diansofdemocracy.com/harris-trump-just-tear-gassed-peac
eful-protesters-for-a-photo-op/.

2 Kamala Harris, "He held up the Bible like it was a Trump
steak," DemocraticUnderground.com, https://www.democrat
icunderground.com/100213539250.

3 Remarks by President Trump at South Dakota's 2020 Mount
Rushmore Fireworks Celebration, The White House, https://
www.whitehouse.gov/briefings-statements/remarks-president
-trump-south-dakotas-2020-mount-rushmore-fireworks-cele
bration-keystone-south-dakota/.

INDEX

Page references for illustrations appear in *italics*